The Open

Book **3** Producing Influential Documents

Prepared for the course team by Jim Donohue,
Lina Adinolfi, David Lewis, Helen Peters and
Prithvi Shrestha

This publication forms part of an Open University course LB160 *Professional communication skills for business studies*. Details of this and other Open University courses can be obtained from the Student Registration and Enquiry Service, The Open University, PO Box 197, Milton Keynes MK7 6BJ, United Kingdom: tel. +44 (0)845 300 60 90; email general-enquiries@open.ac.uk

Alternatively, you may visit the Open University website at www.open.ac.uk where you can learn more about the wide range of courses and packs offered at all levels by The Open University.

To purchase a selection of Open University course materials visit www.ouw.co.uk, or contact Open University Worldwide, Michael Young Building, Walton Hall, Milton Keynes MK7 6AA, United Kingdom for a brochure: tel. +44 (0)1908 858793; fax +44 (0)1908 858787; email ouw-customer-services@open.ac.uk

The Open University

Walton Hall, Milton Keynes

MK7 6AA

First published 2008. Second edition 2009

Edited and designed by The Open University.

Typeset by Pam Callow, S&P Enterprises Ltd, Lydbrook, Glos. GL17 9PP.

Printed in the United Kingdom by Cambrian Printers, Aberystwyth

ISBN 978 0 7492 2543 8

2.1

The paper used in this publication contains pulp sourced from forests independently certified to the Forest Stewardship Council (FSC) principles and criteria.
Chain of custody certification allows the pulp from these forests to be tracked to the end use. (see www.fsc-uk.org).

FSC
Mixed Sources
Product group from well-managed forests and other controlled sources
Cert no. TT-COC-2200
www.fsc.org
© 1996 Forest Stewardship Council

Contents

5

The course team

Lina Adinolfi (author)

Haider Ali (OU Business School adviser)

Liz Benali (course manager)

Jim Donohue (course team chair)

Elizabeth J. Erling (course team member)

Helen Peters (author)

Prithvi Shrestha (author)

Production team

Mandy Anton (graphic designer)

Ann Carter (print buyer)

Peter Lee (editor)

Jon Owen (graphic artist)

Simon Rodwell (media project manager)

Amanda Smith (editor)

Nikki Tolcher (media assistant)

Consultant authors

Derek Davies (University of Manchester)

David Lewis (DML Communication Services, The Netherlands)

External assessor

George Blue (University of Southampton)

Critical readers

Olwyn Alexander (Heriot-Watt University)

Dennis Beer (B200 tutor)

David Hann (E301 and E303 tutor)

Malcolm Harris (B200 tutor)

Mary Lewis (B200 tutor)

Peter Martin (B200 tutor)

Brian Terry (B200 tutor)

Geraldine Wooley (B200 tutor)

We would like to thank the following former B200 students for their contribution to the course design:

Dimitri Billaud

Vera Brenner

Carmen Jaffke

Klaus Konwalin

Gareth Price

Jitendra Ranpura

Caroline Siddall

Tibebu Tefeta

Thanks also go to the following business school students for giving us permission to use their assignments as examples of good practice:

Wayne Barker

Anne Buckingham

Rebecca Britain

Rebecca Chadwick

Assumpta Corley

Lee Farndon

Nicola Fink

Stephanie Firth

Jenny Frister

Ruth Fulton

Rupert Groves

Claire Houlden

Emma Kingston

Tom Laverick

John Lyons

Daniel McCarthy

Nicola McKee

Damian Millington

Ian Pegg

Noel Rafferty

David Sharp

Yoshie Shinoyama

Jenny Sprackling

Martin Surrey

Angela Temple

Christine Thomas

Amanda Todd

Pamela Vang

Debbie Walker

SESSION 1 **What is an influential document?**

1.1 Introduction

Any document you write can be an influential document – from the shortest email to the longest academic essay or business report. You will know whether it is influential by the way your readers respond. In this book, you will concentrate on how the documents you write can influence the people who read them.

The texts you will work with in this part of the course can generally be called 'reports'. Broadly, this book deals with two types of report: in the first half, academic reports; in the second half, workplace reports.

Business studies students are expected to work with texts from both academic and workplace situations and to produce texts which combine academic and workplace styles. For this reason, a third type of report is introduced in this session: one that is written for a business studies course but in a workplace style. Influencing readers in an academic situation requires a different sort of writing from that which influences readers in a workplace situation.

In this book, you will develop your communication skills for academic and workplace writing. The emphasis will be on how this writing influences people. The secret of it is to understand your audience: to know what they know, to anticipate what they expect, and to communicate in a style which fits with their style. This is the approach to communication which has been presented and practised throughout this course. Influential reports are different from successful essays, and influential workplace texts are different from successful academic texts – but they are not **completely** different.

Knowing what is the same and what is different is the ultimate professional communication skill.

Learning outcomes

In this session you will:

- increase your awareness of the similarities and the differences between reports and essays
- identify some features of organisation and language style that make a workplace report influential
- identify some features of organisation and language style that make an academic report influential
- begin to develop a research procedure for writing influential reports
- begin to develop the skill of adapting the organisation and language of academic texts to workplace audiences.

1.2   Documents in different environments

The term *influential documents* used in this book's title refers very broadly to 'reports'. But it also refers to other kinds of texts in academic and work environments, such as self-assessment forms or promotional literature. In effect, it refers to almost any text you might write that is not an essay.

The first activity introduces this range of texts by asking you to identify some that you have previously read or written.

Activity 1.1 ....

Purpose: to raise awareness of texts you have read or written.

Task: create a table with the headings below. In it write the types of document you have read or written. The list below the table gives some examples. Include any other documents that you have read or written which are not in the list.

Academic environment		Work environment		Private environment	
Read	Written	Read	Written	Read	Written

agenda	STEP analysis	progress report	contract
evaluation of a product	recommendation report	proposal	medical report
school report	market research report	annual report	staff appraisal report
credit report	research report	stakeholder analysis	evaluation of proposal
cost–benefit analysis	bid	minutes of a meeting	presentation to a committee
job application letter	feasibility study	personal skills audit	letter to an official agency

There is no answer for this activity because it is personal to you.

Comment

Documents differ in appearance, organisation, style of language, and production process. They are designed differently because they have different purposes and audiences. When designed well, a document has the effects on the audience that the writer intended. It will be **influential**.

In later sessions, you will work with some of the other types of text in the list. But here you will focus on those which are most obviously 'reports'. Before moving on to the next activity, tick each text in your table that is a report.

1.3 Comparing reports and essays

There are similarities and differences between workplace reports and academic reports and between reports and essays. In order to focus on the characteristics of a report, in the next activity you will compare them with essays.

Activity 1.2

Purpose: to introduce the characteristics of reports.

Task 1: create a table with the headings below. Write down some of the ways in which reports and essays differ from each other. An example is done to get you started.

Report	Essay
Written in academic environments **and** workplace environments	Written mainly in academic environments

Task 2: Text 1.1 in Resource Book 3 lists the characteristics of reports and essays but they are mixed up and some are not in the correct column. Use Text 1.1 to help you add to your table any characteristics that you have not already thought of. Remember that the characteristics in Text 1.1 may not be in the correct column.

Compare your answers with those suggested in the Answer section.

Comment

This activity highlights the differences between reports and essays. However, reports are so important in business that some business studies courses don't mind if students' essays look like reports. It is important to find out what your tutor thinks.

Although this activity refers to reports in general, in this session you will work with three different kinds of report. The two main kinds are academic reports and workplace reports. Both kinds report research and may even contain recommendations. But academic reports are written to develop a student's understanding of business, whereas workplace reports are usually designed to influence business colleagues and prompt them into taking some kind of action.

There is a third kind of report which combines the two main types. Sometimes business studies students are asked to write assignments as if the audience are colleagues in a company and not the tutor. This kind of academic report combines the organisation and the style of the other two types.

Finally, although reports and essays are different types of text, they also have many similarities. So, many of the communication skills that you use in producing a successful essay are the same as you use to produce an influential report.

For the rest of this session, you will study aspects of the organisation and the language style of three reports: a workplace report, an academic report, and an academic report written as if it were a workplace report. As you work through these reports, similarities with what you have already studied in this course and differences that you will need to take into account to produce influential documents should become clearer.

1.4 Influential writing in the workplace

Communication in the workplace

Management, marketing, economics, training – almost every aspect of business is concerned with the way organisations, individuals, economies and markets influence each other. *Influence* is *power* and businesses depend on it to turn ideas into activity. Without power businesses would be 'talking shops' – places where ideas are produced but nothing else. The purpose of business communication is to provide information, opinion and argument which can be used as the basis of action: in other words, to inform decision making.

Businesses are actually 'flows of information' and, as communications technology progresses, information is becoming the main commodity that businesses deal with. This can be seen clearly in the financial sector. Most financial staff never see actual money, gold, or stocks and shares. They see **information** about 'financial products'. This information is communicated around the organisation and to other organisations. 'The money markets' are places where information and opinion are exchanged, not physical products.

In such a world of information flows, effective communication is also central. Traditionally, effective communication was seen as a process in which information is shot like an arrow from a transmitter to a receiver (Figure 1.1). It was thought that, as long as the information was clear and concise, the shooting was accurate and nothing got in the way of the speeding information, then communication would be effective.

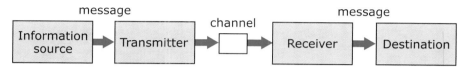

Figure 1.1   Shannon and Weaver's model of communication (Source: adapted from Shannon and Weaver, 1949)

As you can see in Figure 1.1, this is a very early model of communication. Transmission models like this are not the models used in modern businesses. Communication involves more than information – it involves people. Sometimes, it may be enough to shoot information at a receiver in its simplest and clearest form. For example, a department secretary may send out a list of dates for departmental meetings in a well-presented list. However, if a member of the department wants to be excused from one of these meetings, it is unlikely that shooting back an arrow of information like the one below will be successful:

> **Unable to attend 15 January**

To be effective, the sender may have to do more: for example, provide an explanation, check whether they are expected to present anything at that meeting, or express regret. It does not take long to see that shooting information at receivers is a limited kind of communication.

One element that is missing from Shannon and Weaver's model is the notion of **influence**. The qualities of accuracy, clarity and precision which the model encourages are undoubtedly influential in many situations. But accuracy and clarity are not enough on their own to make all communication influential. For communication to be influential, it also needs to persuade people.

A workplace report

In this section you will look at an example of a workplace report that is short and relatively simple. At first it may seem to be rather like an arrow of information. However, even a text as simple as this is only influential if it is designed well for its context. Later in this book, you will study more sophisticated workplace texts.

In the next activity, you will see two versions of the text – an effective one and a non-effective one. The purpose of the activity is to identify specifically what makes one of these versions effective.

Activity 1.3 ....

Purpose: to begin thinking about what makes business writing influential.

Task 1: look fairly quickly at Texts 1.2 and 1.3 in Resource Book 3. Identify which text is likely to be more influential. Note down two or three features which helped you decide.

Task 2: why has the title of the report in Text 1.3 been changed and why have other headings been introduced?

Task 3: why are paragraphs 4 and 5 in Text 1.3 in a different order from Text 1.2?

Task 4: why has the idea in line 16 of Text 1.2 been moved to the end of paragraph 4 in Text 1.3?

Task 5: why have the words *Which doesn't make sense* been removed from paragraph 3 of Text 1.3?

Task 6: paragraph 4 of Text 1.3 and paragraph 5 of Text 1.2 deal generally with the same ideas. Do you think the way these ideas are linked in Text 1.3 is better than the way they are linked in paragraph 5 of Text 1.2? if so, why?

Task 7: the words below from Text 1.2 are not used in Text 1.3. Find which words are used instead and explain why they were changed.

Line 2: *asked us to look into the situation and give our feedback*.

Line 4: *we wanted to see what is going on and we wanted to get very clear about this.*

Line 13: *This is the solution* ...

Task 8: which **six words** are used in Text 1.3 to sum up **all the actions** in the following lines of Text 1.2?

Line 5: (*decided to interview*); line 6 (*sent out questionnaires*); line 7 (*talked to Mrs P*); lines 7–8 (*went and looked in the restaurant several times*); line 8 (*looked at lots of kitchen equipment*).

Task 9: there are several shortened word forms in Text 1.2, such as *can't* and *don't.* Are there any in Text 1.3? Why?

Task 10: in Text 1.2, the writer frequently uses the **personal pronouns** *we, us* and *you.* In Text 1.3, these words are not used at all. The following ideas come from Text 1.2 and all contain personal pronouns. What has the writer of Text 1.3 written to avoid using each of these personal pronouns?

Line 2: *The Managing Director had asked us*

Line 5: *We decided to interview some of the staff*

Line 6: *We sent out questionnaires*

Line 7: *We talked to Mrs P and her team*

Lines 7–8: *We also made sure we went and looked in the restaurant several times.*

Line 8–9: *We looked at lots of kitchen equipments*.

Line 16: *If you aren't careful, you'll lose all the custumers.*

Task 11: the following evaluations from Text 1.2 have been revised in Text 1.3. How and why?

Line 10: *Which doesn't make sense.*

Line 13: *You've got to improve the quality of food.*

Line 15: *What about a second queaue with a different cash register.*

Line 17: *You can't runs a kitchen like this.*

Line 18: *that's got to stop.*

Task 12: find and correct the grammatical mistakes in the following lines of Text 1.2. Try to explain what is wrong with them.

Line 2; line 4; line 6; line 9; line 14; line 17.

Task 13: what is wrong with the second sentence in line 10 of Text 1.2?

Task 14: find and correct the spelling mistakes in the following lines of Text 1.2:

line 6; line 13; line 15; line 16; line 18.

Compare your answers with those suggested in the Answer section.

Task 15: on the basis of your comparison of Texts 1.2 and 1.3, draw up a checklist of basic criteria for producing simple, influential documents in the workplace.

Task 16: what other features of influential documents has this activity not addressed and which are not yet included in your checklist?

There are no answers for Tasks 15 and 16 because they are personal to you.

Comment ....

Reports such as the report on the staff restaurant are designed to be read quickly and efficiently. They must be understood accurately as decisions are based on what they contain. To ensure they are effective, their organisation and language style is clear, concise and impersonal. Mostly, this is a simple factual report of the research methods and the findings. However, the facts are organised in such a way that the recommendations follow logically and the facts seem to 'speak for themselves'. Of course, facts do not actually speak for themselves, as Text 1.2 demonstrates. Even short, reasonably straightforward texts can have an organisation and a language style which is either influential or not.

You may think that the language style of Text 1.3 is too formal and impersonal. The general trend in modern business communication is towards more informal and more personal styles of communication. Some observers call this more informal business style **the conversationalisation of official discourse** (see, for example, Fairclough, 1992 in the References). It is sometimes seen as a way of disguising the power relationships that actually exist.

Whether organisations really are more personal is not so much the point for this course. The issue is how people communicate within a particular company. Texts 1.2 and 1.3 are at two extremes. To communicate influentially depends on moving between these two extremes and finding the right balance of formality and informality to persuade readers in your particular situation.

1.5 An influential document checklist

Writing influentially is a result of practice and experience. To support the practice in this book, an Influential Document Checklist has been drawn up, based on the experience of many writers. This checklist is in the Appendix. It will remind you of the main features of influential documents and your tutor will also use it to evaluate the texts you write.

The checklist deals with five aspects of an influential document: research, text organisation, language style, efficiency and presentation.

It has seven sections, as follows.

A   **The research process** Were the research procedures appropriate for the task, carried out correctly, and have they produced relevant information?

B   **Organisation of the text** Is the structure of the text clear and appropriate to the task and the context?

C   **Language of the subject** Is the language appropriate for the subject of the text?

D   **Language of the relationship with readers** Is the language appropriate for the audience and the reader-writer relationship?

E   **Language of text organisation** Does the language reinforce the organisation of the text?

F   **Clarity, accuracy, conciseness** Is the document efficient?

G   **Qualities of presentation** Are grammar, spelling and word-processing accurate?

In the checklist, each section contains several more detailed criteria. These criteria are introduced and explained further during this book. The next activity begins that process.

Activity 1.4   ....

Purpose: to introduce the Influential Document Checklist.

Task: look back at Tasks 1–14 in Activity 1.3 and at the seven sections (A–G) of the checklist above. Which section does each task in Activity 1.3 deal with? (You **do not** need to look at the full checklist in the Appendix for this activity.)

Compare your answers with those suggested in the Answer section.

Comment   ....

As you study this book you will see it is important to relate the checklist to your experience and, if necessary, to modify the criteria to your own situation.

1.6 Organisation and structure of a report

The structure of research-based reports is familiar to the people who use them. Section B of the Influential Document Checklist refers to this knowledge:

> **B   Organisation of the text** Is the structure of the text clear and appropriate to the task and the context?

The next activity introduces the structure of research-based reports. It deals with both workplace and academic reports.

Activity 1.5 ....

Purpose: to become familiar with the more common sections of a research-based report.

Task: read Text 1.5 in Resource Book 3, which lists all the possible sections of a research-based report. Not every report includes all these sections. But many reports include some of them.

Use the grid below to identify how Text 1.3, 'Report on the service provided by the staff restaurant', is organised. Tick which sections are used and which are not. Tick which sections contain the kind of information suggested in Text 1.5.

Element of report	Text 1.3	Contains information suggested in Text 1.5?
Memo or covering letter		
Title page		
Executive summary or abstract		
Contents page		
Terms of reference or Introduction		
Review of literature		
Method		
Measurement criteria		
Results or Findings		
Discussion		
Conclusion(s)		
Recommendation(s)		
Bibliography or References		
Appendices		
Glossary		

Compare your answers with those suggested in the Answer section.

Comment ....

Text 1.5 includes every section that could be used to organise a research-based report. In both workplace and academic environments, decisions have to be made about whether each section is necessary, whether sections should be combined, and how much information to include in each section. These decisions have to be based on your understanding of your audience. You have looked at the way one particular workplace report was organised. In the next section, you will do the same with an academic report.

1.7 An academic report

Before moving on, we should summarise what has already been established about *workplace reports*:

They are texts which describe and analyse a situation, on the basis of research, in response to a need or request. They probably include recommendations and are structured for efficiency.

Academic reports at undergraduate level are more likely to be in response to an assignment title. The purpose of the title is to encourage students to learn more about an area of business studies and to apply that knowledge to business situations.

In this section you will be introduced to the organisation of an academic report. This report is studied in greater detail in Session 2, so you do not need to read it closely in this session.

Activity 1.6 ....

Purpose: to identify the structure of an academic report.

Task 1: read the assignment title at the beginning of Text 1.6 in Resource Book 3. Then read quickly through Text 1.6 and tick any sections of a research-based report structure you can see in the grid below.

Element of report	In Text 1.6?
Title page	
Executive summary or abstract	
Contents page	
Terms of reference or Introduction	
Review of literature	
Method	
Measurement criteria	
Results or Findings	
Discussion	
Conclusion(s)	
Recommendation(s)	
Bibliography or References	
Appendices	
Glossary	

Task 2: the student who wrote Text 1.6 created a report structure which is adapted to the task set in the assignment. On a separate sheet of paper, draw a plan of how Text 1.6 is organised. To help you identify the main sections of this report use the headings in Text 1.6,

the section headings in the table above, and any other information you can obtain from Text 1.6.

Compare your answers with those suggested in the Answer section.

Comment ....

The structure of this academic report is a response to the assignment task and the audience – that is, the course tutor – and was evaluated by the tutor as highly successful. This is because the report successfully applies the concepts from a business studies course to a business situation. This is one of the main purposes of this kind of report in an academic environment. However, such a report might not be so influential in a workplace environment. Although it is structured into sections, it is not as easy to identify quickly what the main points of the report are as it was for Text 1.3.

For this session, Text 1.6 was used to highlight how the different purposes of academic and workplace reports affect the way they are structured. In the final section of this session, you will look at how to write a report for workplace and academic purposes combined.

1.8 An academic report to influence two audiences

Terms of reference

As you saw in Section 1.7, business studies reports, like workplace reports, present the results of an investigation and are written to influence an audience. However, as you have also seen, there are some differences between what influences a course tutor and what influences readers in a workplace. To give students practice in communicating with workplace audiences, some business studies assignments ask them to write a report **as if** it is for a workplace audience. In this section, you will look at such an assignment.

The assignment comes from the marketing section of a business studies course. Students were given a short case study of an organisation which runs theme parks and leisure activities called Grand Days Out plc. The next activity looks at the terms of reference for the report.

Activity 1.7 ....

Purpose: to establish the terms of reference for a report.

Task 1: read the guidance notes for the assignment title below and complete the following table.

Terms of reference

Subject matter	
Aim	
Audience	

Guidance notes

Assignment title

Produce a short report that will help the participants in a staff training day understand how older consumers are likely to decide to visit a Grand Days Out (GDO) theme park.

For this assignment you should concentrate especially on applying models and concepts from the course. An appreciation of how organisations maintain relationships and communicate with their customers (gained from your study of the course) will help produce a strong answer. Try to concentrate on what marketing can contribute to understanding the decision-making processes that customers go through.

You need to keep in mind the audience for your work and ensure it is rigorously presented. You are required to write a **short report**. This may need one or more subheadings for clarity.

Although the scenario involves a presentation to a group of colleagues, you can assume your audience would like to know the sources of any models, quotations and theories that you refer to, so include references in your report where appropriate. However, your tutor will expect clear information and explanations that non-specialists can use to understand the marketing and planning processes that affect them.

Compare your answer with that suggested in the Answer section.

Comment ....

As with the academic report in the previous section, students are expected to use concepts from the business studies course in writing the report. At the same time, the assignment asks them to imagine that they are writing the report to be given out at a workplace staff training day. This means they are really trying to write for two audiences at the same time – their tutor, who is an academic specialist, and the imaginary workplace audience, who may have different kinds of knowledge.

Content (or subject matter)

In the next two activities you will think about the assignment title before you look at some students' writing.

Activity 1.8

Purpose: to activate your background knowledge about the assignment.

Task: In the middle of a blank piece of paper, write the words 'Theme park'. Then write any ideas around these words that come into your mind about theme parks. If you are not sure what a theme park is, or you do not have any experience of a theme park, search the internet to find a few ideas. At this stage, it is not important which ideas you find – they are all useful.

There is no answer for this activity because it is personal to you.

Comment

The purpose of this activity is to activate some of your ideas about theme parks. If you look at their publicity material, you will see many references to children. Young people are important users of theme parks. However, the assignment title asks you to think about a different user group – older people. How might older people decide to have a day out at a theme park?

Activity 1.9

Purpose: to activate your thoughts about why older people might decide to visit a theme park.

Task: on a second sheet of paper write down any reasons why older people might decide to visit a theme park. Also write down any reasons why they would not want to. Then write down any thoughts you have about what a theme park company would have to do in order to encourage more older people to visit. What changes or new features would the theme park have to introduce?

Again, there is no answer for this activity.

Comment

These two activities were designed as preparation for reading the student report in the next three activities. It should be easier to read a text when you already have some thoughts about its topic.

The comments below from two tutors refer to the difficulty of engaging with workplace audiences in a student assignment.

1 You have done very well with the theory and have clearly learned a lot in writing this assignment. However, the language you use in this report may not be very easy for the Grand Days Out staff to understand. You have presented the ideas and theory mostly in academic language. This impresses me, your tutor. But you need to express these ideas in more everyday language which will appeal to the staff.

2 This report is based on a very good understanding of the source material by Blythe and you have referenced it well. You do address the Grand Days Out audience directly but you could get them more involved if you used some more motivational language.

The two comments refer to two aspects of language style which are not academic. The first one asks for a more straightforward and less technical language style. The second refers to 'motivational language', which is a more emotional and involving language style. These differences in language style relate to two different sections of the Influential Document Checklist. More straightforward and less technical language is referred to in Section C, *The language of the field*. More emotional and involving language is referred to in Section D, *The language of the relationship*. To communicate successfully in this report, students need to adapt their academic style in both these respects.

Organisation and structure

The next two activities look at how a student (Rosa) uses an academic business studies model called the 'consumer decision-making process' to organise her report.

Activity 1.10 ....

Purpose: to introduce the 'consumer decision-making process' that Rosa uses to frame her report.

Task 1: Extract 1.7 in Resource Book 3 is an academic diagram representing the 'consumer decision-making process'. Below are some statements made by a visitor to a theme park. Number the visitor's statements so that they are in the same order as the process shown in Extract 1.7. The first one is done for you as an example. Some of the concepts in the diagram may be unfamiliar. Don't worry about this: use any technique, such as using a dictionary or guessing, to match the statements with the diagram.

I'd like two tickets for a day at the Grand Days Out Theme Park.

I must tell all my friends about this and go again as soon as I can.

What's on offer?

Well, let's see. Did I enjoy it?

How do the prices, amusements, travel costs and everything else compare?

[1] I need a day out.

Compare your answers with those suggested in the Answer section.

Comment ....

This activity introduced the concepts of the decision-making process by converting them into the everyday language of a customer. The next activity looks at how business studies concepts like these can be used to organise a workplace report

Activity 1.11 ....

Purpose: to note how a report is organised using business studies concepts.

Task: Text 1.8 in Resource Book 3 is the text of Rosa's report. The discussion section was originally organised in the same order as the stages in the decision-making process (Extract 1.7). However, for this activity, the paragraphs in the discussion section of the text are mixed up. Use Extract 1.7 to help you number the paragraphs so they are in the right order. There are four gaps where Rosa originally included the name of the stage. Write in what you think the missing words are. Paragraphs 1 and 2 and the conclusion are in the right order.

Compare your answer with that suggested in the Answer section.

Comment

Text 1.9 in Resource Book 3 is the report in its original order. The organisation of this report is relatively simple. It begins with an Introduction to the topic and makes clear what the aim of the report is. The main body of the report, headed 'The consumer decision-making process', is a Discussion section. There are no practical research findings and the discussion is based entirely on applying a set of concepts from a business model to the business situation. There are no subheadings but it is possible to head each section of the Discussion with the concept words from the decision-making process diagram. Finally, there is a Conclusion which relates the Discussion back to the topic of the report and of the staff training day (which Rosa calls *the Ideas Generation Day*).

This report shows how academic concepts can provide a structure for a report. Business studies frameworks and models like this can help professional communication in the workplace.

However, the generalisations of the academic model will not interest or influence a workplace audience if they cannot be related to the actual experience of customers. The academic model is designed to generalise about the decision-making process, so it is written in abstract academic language that does this. The visitor to the theme park is talking about their particular situation and uses language that expresses personal experience. To be influential in the workplace, the language style of academic models usually has to be adapted to a workplace audience.

Engaging with the audience

The difficulty with referring to 'a workplace audience' is that there are very many different workplace audiences. These can range from highly informed specialists in the subject you are communicating about to totally non-informed non-specialists.

Influential documents need to be written quite differently for different audiences across this range. Referring to the Influential Document Checklist, this means making decisions about the language in Section C – on the subject matter of the text – and Section D – for creating the relationship with the audience. To make these decisions you have to know your audience, what they know and what style is most likely to communicate with them. Then you can decide where you want your text to be on the following scales.

Academic	-----------------------------------	Non-academic
Specialist	-----------------------------------	Non-specialist
Formal	-----------------------------------	Non-formal
Impersonal	-----------------------------------	Personal
Indirect	-----------------------------------	Direct
Abstract	-----------------------------------	Concrete
Written style	-----------------------------------	Spoken style

Some workplace texts are just as academic, specialist and formal as university essays – they belong towards the left-hand end of these scales. Others belong towards the right-hand end. Their writers have adapted the texts to suit their imagined audience. If you are interested in seeing an example of professional writers who have adapted their texts to suit different imagined audiences, read Texts 1.10 and 1.11 in Resource Book 3. These are both analysis texts written by economists working in commercial banks. Where would you place each text on the scales above? Which language features helped you decide?

When the Good Days Out assignment asks you to imagine the audience you are writing for, you are doing exactly what professional writers do. In order to produce the text, you have to imagine the audience and choose a writing style that suits them. This means moving to the right or the left on each of the scales above.

The next activity looks at five language features which a student used to adapt an academic style to the workplace audience they have imagined in the Good Days Out company.

Activity 1.12

Purpose: to introduce some language features for adapting an academic text to influence a workplace audience.

Task 1: look again at the guidance notes in Activity 1.8. Think about the audience for this report. Look at the style scales above and decide what would be the appropriate communication styles for this audience.

Task 2: the tutors' comments suggested that the report should be written in a motivational style. Look at Extracts A and B below. Which one is likely to be more motivational for the GDO audience? Underline the language features which make you think this.

Extract A	Extract B
Once the key decision maker for entertainment purchases in the family has been identified, they can be targeted by the providing organisation. It seems likely that children or parents will be the decision makers. It seems unlikely that grandparents will be; they seem more likely to consume theme park entertainment incidentally as a result of their accompanying the primary consumers in the family.	Once we know for sure which member of the family takes the decision to go to a theme park then we are able to start targeting that individual. Children or parents are most likely to make these decisions. Grandparents are not. They are most likely to be 'dragged' there by the parents or children.

Compare your answers with those suggested in the Answer section.

Comment

It is important to note that the student has **imagined** her audience. It is not very clear from the guidance notes how specialised the GDO audience is. The student has chosen to write in a very non-specialist style and to express a high level of solidarity with her readers. She does this by moving away from some of the typical features of academic writing, towards a more spoken style. However, workplace texts are not necessarily more spoken. The report on the staff restaurant is an example of a very formal, written workplace document. Therefore, it is not correct to say that all workplace reports move towards the right-hand end of the scales above and academic reports move towards the left. But it is important to know which language features move a document one way or the other along the scales and which will be more or less influential with your audience. In some ways, this is more difficult with these hybrid academic/workplace reports than it is with pure workplace or academic reports.

Activity 1.13   ....

Purpose: to note how Rosa's report engages with the GDO audience.

Task: look through Text 1.9 and highlight any sentences which show that Rosa is attempting to write for an audience that is not academic.

Compare your answer with that suggested in the Answer section.

Comment   ....

In places, Rosa uses language that is deliberately designed to relate academic concepts to the life experience of customers and of the workplace audience. To a certain extent she uses a more direct spoken style to do this. However, she does not go too far in this direction. She is still producing a written text and real spoken language would not be influential in such a document. She simply mixes some features of spoken language into her written text.

Activity 1.14   ....

Purpose: to practise adapting a text to a particular workplace audience.

Task: use the five features of a less academic style given in the answer to Activity 1.13 to rewrite the extracts below in language more likely to influence the Good Days Out audience.

Extract C

During the problem recognition stage of the process the customer will be conscious that they have a need for a particular service or product. The needs of a customer at this stage can be categorised as either utilitarian (concerned with the practical, functional attributes of the product) or hedonic (concerned with the pleasurable or aesthetic aspect of the product) (Blythe, 2005, p. 45). In the context of the service provided by GDO, the focus should be on responding to the hedonic needs of a customer.

Extract D

Creating the right product for the targeted older demographic is not enough. GDO must gain mind share of the older age range by reaching the segment through the most effective media. GDO must provide exceptional customer service levels during the buying transaction, the actual experience, and the follow-up to encourage repeat purchase.

Compare your answers with those suggested in the Answer section.

Comment ....

The purpose of these activities is to highlight the relationship between the audience, the purpose and the language of the text. Often, the relatively objective, impersonal and written style of academic writing is also appropriate for much workplace writing. The most influential features of any text are that it is clearly organised and efficiently expressed. However, because academic writing has a purpose which is less connected to decision making and action, it can be less direct and more abstract than some workplace writing and therefore seem less efficient than it should be. In both academic and workplace writing, professional communication skill means finding the right position somewhere between the extremes of the style scales for the audience you imagine will read your text.

This section of Session 1 introduced the criteria in Sections B, C and D of the Influential Document Checklist: the organisation of the text using academic concepts; the choice of vocabulary for talking about the subject matter; and the language of the relationship with the reader. The next section turns to a different part of the checklist.

1.9 Time frames, actions and verbs

One of the language features referred to in the final section of the Influential Document Checklist is correct grammar. Workplace writing is sometimes said to focus more on action and, therefore, the grammar is more verb-based, while academic writing is more focused on ideas and, therefore, the grammar is more noun-based. This is an oversimplification but this session on report writing ends by reviewing the grammar of verbs and time in reports.

When you want to express time in reports, there are four choices to make. For each choice you change the form of the verb. The four choices are introduced below.

Past or present tense

The grammar of verbs can show whether the time of the action (such as *began*) or state (such as *is*) is past (*began*) or present (*is*).

Progressive or non-progressive

The grammar of verbs can show whether the action or state continues through a time period (in other words, is **progressive**, like *was producing*) or happens at a point in time (in other words, is **non-progressive**, like *bought*).

Perfect or non-perfect

The grammar of verbs can show whether the action or state occurs in a time period leading up to another point in time (that is, **past perfect**, like *had become*, or **present perfect**, like *has developed*) or happens at a point in time (for example, the **past simple**, like *bought*).

Modal or non-modal

This session deals only with the two modal verbs *will* and *shall* which are used in combination with other verbs to refer to future time.

These are the four main choices you need to make when using verbs to talk about time. There are usually other words in a sentence which also refer to time (for example, *back in 1950*). These work together with the verbs to make clear to a reader the timing of actions or states in the document. Influential documents should be clear about timing.

Texts 1.12 and 1.13 in Resource Book 3 are the timeline for a company and show how the company has developed over the past 100 years. Nearly all the possible verb forms which could be used to write about this development are included in Text 1.13. The position of each verb along the timeline shows what part of the time frame the verb refers to. Text 1.12 is the same timeline but without the verbs.

Activity 1.15 ....

Purpose: to focus on how verb forms communicate time.

Task: First look at Text 1.13 as revision. Then fill in the gaps in Text 1.12 using one of the following verbs: *expand*, *work*, *launch*, *start*, *move*, *found*, *enter*, *lead*, *operate*, *do*, *be*, *make*, *continue*, *produce*, *have*.

Compare your answers with the timeline in Text 1.13.

Activity 1.16 ....

Purpose: to revise the verb tenses.

Task: complete the following sentences with the appropriate verb tenses of those given in brackets.

1   Throughout the 1990s inflation (be) fairly low and stable, but it (increase) since 2001.

2   Oil prices (decrease) slowly since they (peak) in 2004.

3   As the demand for commodities (grow), the world economy (become) stronger.

4   In a study carried out last year, the IMF (predict) that the price of gold (fall) by $10.

5   If Germany's current unemployment rates (increase) further, it will cause even more instability.

6   Unemployment figures (seem) to (decrease) in Sweden due to a decrease in individuals' working hours.

7   The value of the US dollar (fall) since 2002.

8   Now the weak dollar (become) a matter of deep economic concern around the world.

9   In the 21st century, the centre of gravity of the global economy (shift) away from the older and established economies of Europe and Japan.

10 The state of the international economy (remain) a worry if the mortgage and debt crisis (continue) ...

11 This major telecommunications company (acquire) two small networks since they (enter) the sector.

12 I recently (acquire) two properties in the north of the town.

Compare your answers with those suggested in the Answer section.

Comment ....

This short section on verb grammar was designed to focus your attention on verbs and time. It might have shown you that you are quite confident about how to use verbs for time-frame management. However, if you found that focusing on verb tenses raised questions for you, it may be useful to pay attention to verb tenses when you edit your writing.

If you would like more practice on verb forms, some useful websites are suggested on the course website.

1.10 Conclusion

Documents are influential if they are appropriate for their purpose and their audience. There is not a single report style or structure which is suitable for every reader in every situation. As you move from situation to situation, reader to reader, and task to task, you are faced with decisions about how to communicate effectively.

But this does not make every situation totally different. A writer who is able to create a clear structure, manage the information load, and adopt an influential language style in one situation has a basis for adapting to other situations. Influential writers are writers who adapt.

In this session, you studied three main types of report. In the remaining sessions you will study reports that are adapted to a range of academic and workplace environments.

1.11 Review

In this session you should have:
- increased your awareness of the similarities and the differences between reports and essays
- identified some features of organisation and language style that make a workplace report influential
- identified some features of organisation and language style that make an academic report influential
- begun to develop a procedure for writing influential reports
- begun to develop the skill of adapting the organisation and language of academic texts to workplace audiences.

1.12 Answer section

Activity 1.2

Report	Essay
Written in academic environments **and** workplace environments	Mainly written in academic environments
Based on data collected from company documents, surveys, questionnaires, work experience: that is, from original, primary sources	Based on other people's research, theories and analysis: that is, on secondary sources written by academic experts
Divided into separate sections	Has continuous paragraphs
Sections have headings, points may be numbered	Does not contain section headings or numbering
Contains tables, charts and appendices	Does not contain tables or appendices (usually)
Normally extremely objective	May include subjective opinion
Information may be repeated in different places in the text	Very little repetition of information
Paragraphs tend to be shorter	Paragraphs tend to be longer
Often recommends action	Does not include recommendations
Includes description of methods used	Does not refer to the research method or how the text was created
Writing style is different in different sections	Writing style is the same throughout

Activity 1.3

Task 2

The word *situation* has been changed to *service* to make the subject of the report more specific and clear. The other headings have been introduced to make the report easier to read by dividing it into sections and giving each section a name.

Task 3

This is now a more logical order. The Conclusions are the summary of the Findings section, which comes before it. The Recommendations grow logically from the Conclusions. In certain reports Recommendations may be moved to the beginning. It depends on the writer's judgement about whether readers are interested in the detailed findings, or whether they trust the writer to make the judgement and will only look at the findings if they need additional information.

Task 4

Because it deals with the effect of the problems listed in the paragraph. It is more logical to have the effect after the cause in this part of the report.

Task 5

The Findings in this report are all facts or data collected in the research. *Which doesn't make sense* is not data or a fact but a judgement or an expression of opinion. If these words are included in the report, they belong in the Conclusions or Recommendations section. (However, they are not an appropriate way to express an opinion.)

Task 6

The ideas are introduced with a statement: *The principal conclusions ... were*. Then each conclusion has the same pattern. It begins with the word *that* followed by a similar group of words:

> that user criticisms were largely justified
>
> that the current single sitting placed impossible demands
>
> that the kitchen equipment currently in use was in urgent need
>
> that the current single user flow-system was a main cause.

This kind of repeated pattern is called **parallelism**. The link between the ideas is created by the parallel pattern in which they are written.

The ideas in paragraph 5 of Text 1.2 are not linked at all. All the sentences are separate.

Task 7

Line 2: *Requested the working party to investigate the nature and quality of the service provided and to make recommendations for improvements.*

Requested is a more formal word for *asked*. *Working party* is more precise than *us*. All the other replacement words are simultaneously more precise and more formal.

Line 4: The next two examples are also more precise and more formal at the same time: *In order to ascertain the precise nature of the service provided identify the specific areas of complaint.* This language is commonly used when writing about investigations where it is important to appear neutral and unemotional about the subject matter. *See what was going on* is an expression often associated with emotional conflict and seems less neutral.

Line 13: *The working party recommends that urgent consideration be given to implementing the following measures.*

This is a very formal way of proposing solutions. But it is also more careful to leave responsibility for the actions with the Managing Director. The working party should make recommendations, not instruct the Director to take a particular course of action.

Task 8

The following investigatory procedures were adopted.

This is more formal but is also a high-level generalisation, which gives a good introduction to the more detailed examples of the procedures in the following sentences.

Task 9

There are no shortened words in Text 1.3 because it contains formal words more suited to formal writing. However, this is changing and some writers do include shortened words such as *can't* and *we'll* in formal text.

Task 10

Line 2: *The Managing Director asked us* becomes *The Managing Director requested the working party*. By using the official name of the group the writer belongs to.

Line 5: *We decided to interview some of the staff* becomes *a cross-section were interviewed*. Using the **passive verb form** means there is no need to say who did the interviewing.

Line 6: *We sent out questionnaires* becomes *Questionnaires were sent out*. As above.

Line 7: *We talked to Mrs P and her team* becomes *The staff restaurant manager, Mrs Patterson, was interviewed*. As above.

Lines 7–8: *We also made sure we went and looked in the restaurant several times* becomes *observations took place*. The action (*observed*) is turned into a noun (*observation*) and combined with the verb *took place* which allows no mention of who carried out the action.

Lines 8–9: *We looked at lots of kitchen equipments* becomes *A range of kitchen equipment was evaluated*. As with the other passive verb forms.

Line 16: *If you aren't careful you'll lose all the custumers* becomes *Failure to introduce corrective measures would almost certainly result in staff finding alternative lunch provisions*. The actions of customers (*finding alternative lunch provisions*) are presented as an impersonal effect (*would almost certainly result in*) of a cause (*failure to introduce corrective measures*). They are not blamed on the company (*If you aren't careful*).

Task 11

Line 10: *Which doesn't make sense*. This judgement has been removed because it was an evaluation in the wrong place in the Findings section.

Line 13: *You've got to improve the quality of food*. This judgement is expressed as strongly but more impersonally by the passive verb form, *must be improved*.

Line 15: *What about a second queaue with a different cash register?* This kind of question which actually hides a statement (*you should have a second queue ...*) is an indirect recommendation more appropriate for conversation where it might be used to avoid being directly critical. In a written report, it is probably seen as more critical because it is indirect.

Line 17: *You can't runs a kitchen like this* is a very direct criticism. Such criticism will be seen as destructive, not constructive, criticism.

Line 18: *that's got to stop* is also a very direct and confrontational instruction. Such instructions are not usually appropriate in a report.

Task 12

Line 2: Managing Director ~~had~~ asked us (time frame of the verb is wrong); line 4: what ~~is~~ was going on (time frame of the verb is wrong); line 6: ~~on~~ about (preposition is wrong); line 9: equipment~~s~~ (*equipment* is a non-count noun and so cannot be made plural by adding an *s*); line 14: some new equipment which ~~it~~ cuts the cost (*which* and *it* are both reference back pronouns. In this case, *which* is correct and *it* is not necessary); line 17: you can't run~~s~~ a kitchen (when the verb *can* is followed by another verb, the second verb does not have an *s*).

Task 13

The second sentence in line 10 of Text 1.2 is not a full sentence because it starts with a reference back pronoun (*which*) that is used to join ideas together inside a sentence, not across two different sentences. So there needs to be a second idea in this sentence. In fact, this idea should be included in the first sentence in line 10.

Task 14

Line 6: questionnaires; line 13: quality; line 15: queue; line 16: customers; line 18: queuing.

Activity 1.4

B **Organisation of the text**: Tasks 2–5 and first item in Task 11.
D **Language of the relationship with readers**: Task 7–11.
E **Language of text organisation**: Task 6.
F **Clarity, accuracy, conciseness**: Tasks 2–6 and 12–14.
G **Qualities of presentation**: Tasks 12–14.

Sections A and C of the checklist are not dealt with in the activity.

Activity 1.5

Element of report	Text 1.3	Contains information suggested in Text 1.5?
Memo or covering letter		
Title page		
Executive summary or abstract		
Contents page		
Terms of reference or Introduction	✓	✓
Review of literature		
Method	✓	✓
Measurement criteria		
Results or Findings	✓	✓
Discussion	✓	✓
Conclusion(s)	✓	✓
Recommendation(s)	✓	✓
Bibliography or References		
Appendices		
Glossary		

Activity 1.6

Task 1

Element of report	Text 1.5
Terms of reference or Introduction	✓
Review of literature	✓
Method	✓
Measurement criteria	
Results or Findings	✓
Discussion	✓
Conclusion	
Recommendations	
Bibliography or References	✓

Task 2

This report does not have many of the sections in Text 1.6 (see list below). But, in general, it is designed like a report rather than an essay.

Introduction – background to the organisation and purpose of report.

Method of analysis – the models to be used.

Findings – the completed diagrams of the models.

Discussion – the Operations Director's role.

Activity 1.7

Terms of reference

Subject matter Generally: (1) an appreciation of how organisations develop and maintain relationships and communicate with their customers (gained from your study of the course); (2) an application of marketing concepts to the decision-making processes that customers go through.

Particularly: how older consumers are likely to decide to visit a GDO theme park.

Aim (1) To demonstrate your knowledge of how course concepts apply to real-life business situations; (2) to present this knowledge in a way that will inform and motivate staff in the GDO company.

Audience The imaginary audience are the participants in a GDO staff training day. The real audience is a business studies tutor who will read the report as if they are a member of the GDO staff.

Activity 1.10

1. I need a day out.
2. What's on offer?
3. How do the prices, amusements, travel costs and everything else compare?
4. I'd like two tickets for a day at the Grand Days Out Theme Park.
5. Well, let's see. Did I enjoy it?
6. I must tell all my friends about this and go again as soon as I can.

Activity 1.11

Paragraph a = 8; b = 10; c = 5 (missing words *an information search*; *search*); d = 12; e = 7; f = 4; g = 9; h = 3 (missing words *problem recognition*); i = 11 (missing word *divestment*); j = 6.

Activity 1.12

Extract A is the more academic of the two extracts. The student has made the following five changes to the language style of Extract B to adapt it to the workplace audience they have imagined. Examples of these changes are highlighted and numbered in the text below.

Extract B

1. Uses the pronouns *we* and *our* to show solidarity with the audience.
2. Uses fewer technical terms or explains the technical terms used.
3. Builds sentences around action verbs rather than long abstract noun phrases.
4. Uses active forms of verbs, not passive forms.
5. Expresses opinions with more certainty.

Extract A	Extract B
Once [3] the key decision maker for entertainment purchases in the family has been identified, they [4] can be targeted by the providing organisation. [5] It seems likely that children or parents will be the decision makers. It seems unlikely that grandparents will be; they seem more likely to consume theme park entertainment incidentally as a result of their accompanying [2] the primary consumers in the family.	Once [1] we know for sure [3] which member of the family takes the decision to go to a theme park then [4] we are able to start targeting that individual. Children or parents [5] are most likely to make these decisions. Grandparents are not. [2] They are most likely to be 'dragged' there by the parents or children.

Activity 1.13

Obviously ... the type of service we are marketing we will be looking to capture ...

It is likely that when one of our potential customers has identified a need it is for a day out somewhere that will provide them with entertainment.

In this case our prospective customer would be remembering any previous involvement they may have had with leisure attractions.

Here our prospective customer might visit a travel agents ...

... they will then make the purchase and participate in their experience with us.

In the case of GDO plc our aim would be that they store their memories happily and want to return at the next opportunity.

We should ensure that as staff of GDO plc we give the customers an opportunity ... to complain or provide us with feedback from their experiences with us. This way the customer is more likely to become a repeat customer as it gives us a chance to put things right before they go away thinking that we do not care. By putting their problems right it shows we do care.

Activity 1.14

Extract C

The first step for a person making a decision to purchase something is that they recognise that there is a problem. In this case a problem means that a person needs a service or product. They either need something practical (which is called a utilitarian need) or they need something pleasurable or aesthetic (which is called a hedonic need) (Blythe, 2005, p. 45). Here at GDO, we should be interested in how we can supply our customers with pleasure.

Extract D

It is not enough for us to just create a product that will appeal to older people. We also need to work out how we can tell them about our products most effectively and which media will help us communicate with them best. We also need to make sure that when they visit our theme parks they really enjoy themselves and want to come back again.

Activity 1.16

1: was; has been increasing, or has increased; 2: have decreased; peaked; 3: the choice depends on the combination of the two verbs. Some possible combinations are grows, becomes/is becoming – has grown, has become/becomes/is becoming – grew, became; 4: predicted; would fall; 5: increase; 6: seemed; to have decreased; 7: has fallen; 8: is becoming, has become; 9: has shifted; 10: will remain; continues; 11: has been acquiring; entered; 12: acquired.

SESSION 2 **Writing an academic report**

2.1 Introduction

In Session 1 you looked at the definition of a report, some possible forms it can take and the various categories that can be used to classify reports and their different components. In this session you will examine the language of reports and ways of presenting information to readers in more detail.

During this session you will be asked to write several fairly short pieces of text based on the models and examples which are discussed. At the end you will be asked to put these texts together to form a report. Your report will be included in the collection of documents which you submit for assessment at the end of this course.

A report may be mainly factual, with the purpose of giving information; it may be instructional, expecting the reader to act on the information provided; or it may be persuasive, aimed at achieving a purpose determined by the writer. If they are successful, all of these can be influential documents.

Learning outcomes

In this session you will:

- apply what you learned in Session 1 about the general characteristics of reports
- examine three different functions of report writing – informing, analysing justifying
- analyse different ways of using grammar to manage information flow
- look at ways of representing information diagrammatically in reports
- discuss aspects of report writing online with fellow students
- write a brief report.

Writing about your environment

The report you will produce at the end of this session will be a response to the following assignment.

> Using the concepts, theories and models from previous sessions as a framework for your thinking, write a description of your organisation in its environment, and the issues that are important to it at the present time. Specify your work role and indicate how it relates to the purpose of the organisation. (If you are not currently employed, you may describe your living environment and your different roles, or your previous experience of a workplace.)

This report will be included in the collection of texts you submit for assessment towards the end of this course. (See the online *Assessment Booklet* for more details on this.) The activities in this session will guide you through writing the report. You will then have an opportunity to send the report to your tutor for feedback. Finally, you will have an opportunity to redraft it and include it with your texts for assessment. When you finally submit it, you will also submit a critical reflection on the process of writing the report.

In Session 1 you looked at a report about a staff restaurant, which described data collected in a workplace, written with the aim of informing the managing director of the findings. You also looked at the overall structure of an academic report written in response to the assignment title above. In Activity 2.1 you will compare that same academic report with another one. These reports are similar to the one you will be asked to produce at the end of this session.

2.2 Overall structure of a report

The principal objective in writing a report is that it should convey the necessary information to achieve its objectives in as clear and straightforward a way as possible. As you saw in Session 1, the overall structure of a report is very important.

Activity 2.1 ....

Purpose: to look at the structure of two sample reports and consider the structure for your own report.

Task 1: look at Texts 2.1 and 2.2 in Resource Book 3 and tick which sections they have in the grid below.

Section	Text 2.1	Text 2.2
Table of contents		
Introduction		
Discussion, under numbered and/or headed sections		
Conclusion		
Recommendations		
References		
Appendices		

Task 2: which report do you think is best structured for its purpose? Why?

Compare your answer to Task 1 with that suggested in the Answer section. Task 2 is discussed in the comment below.

Comment

Modern technology makes it easy for documents to be made attractive with photographs or drawings but this is not necessary and, in the academic context, not recommended. Later you will study reports in which visual representations are important to the meaning but, in this case, the visual adds nothing to the information content of the report. In Text 2.1 there is a contents page and information is organised under clear headings. There is a conclusion but no introduction or reference list, although the writer refers to Porter (1980) in the report.

Text 2.2 does not have a title page, a contents page or a conclusion but it does have references. The information is clearly organised under headings but it needs a conclusion to sum up and briefly comment on the overall content. As mentioned in Session 1, in a workplace environment, Text 2.2 might be more clearly divided into subsections to allow the reader to find information in it more quickly.

2.3 Functions of a report (1): giving information

Session 1 was a general introduction to the structure of a research-based report. In this session, you will look more closely at how it is organised. In particular, you will concentrate on the way a report is organised to fulfil three functions:

- giving information
- analysing
- explaining and justifying.

Much of what you do in this session relates to Sections B and E of the Influential Document Checklist, so you may find it helpful to refer to the checklist in the Appendix as you work through this session.

This section introduces the descriptive component of a report. This presents information in a neutral way to give the reader an overview of the situation. You will have seen from the two examples that Text 2.1 includes a section entitled 'Background' about the organisation where the writer works. Text 2.2 does this in the 'Introduction'.

You will also need to start your report by giving some background for the readers – your tutor and your fellow students – on the assumption that they know very little about where you work and what you do. You will have a choice about how you present your environment. You may want to present it in a very positive way, either because you are very happy with it or because you feel it is inappropriate for you to make any critical comments. On the other hand, you may prefer to be critical about certain aspects of your environment, if you think this will be useful and constructive, possibly in bringing about change. You can see examples of different approaches to this in Extracts 2.3 and 2.4 in Resource Book 3. (These are extracts from Texts 2.1 and 2.2.)

Activity 2.2 ....

Purpose: to judge the overall effect of two texts.

Task: read Extracts 2.3 and 2.4 in Resource Book 3. Then consider the following questions.

- Do you prefer one extract to the other? If so, why?
- Do you think one extract is more effective or informative than the other? Why?
- Do they appear to be addressed to similar or different audiences?
- If different, how?
- Would you describe one as more formal than the other? Why?
- Do you think each writer is expressing a personal view of the organisation or being purely factual?
- If you think there is an evaluative element, what view is being expressed?

Compare your answers with those suggested in the Answer section.

Comment ....

Writers adapt their approach according to their audience and what information they want to convey to them. In Extract 2.3 the writer seems to be promoting the organisation she works for, whereas in Extract 2.4 the writer is more focused on how his organisation could be improved. These aspects of influential writing are addressed in Section D of the Influential Writing Checklist, the reader–writer relationship. Think about the approach you will take when describing your organisation.

The relationship you set up with your reader is an important part of presenting information effectively. It is called **relationship management**. Equally important is **information management**. The two are closely connected. How you organise the information in your report depends on your ideas about what your readers already know and are interested in. The following activities look more closely at how information is structured in the report.

Managing information flow in a report

In academic reports, the writer's aim is generally to present the information in an unbiased form, without referring to individuals or implicating responsibilities. To do this, an influential writer exploits an important way of conveying meaning in English. This is through **word order**. Writers choose the order of words in a sentence with a particular aim in mind and this affects the message. This aspect of report writing is covered in Section E of the Influential Document Checklist. It is studied further below.

Theme and point

Book 2 Session 3 introduced the concepts of **theme** and **point**. It explained how an essay, a paragraph and a sentence all have a theme. This is also important in report writing. The title and the introduction of a report give the theme for the whole piece of writing. At the start of a paragraph or section a theme is introduced, after which the theme of each sentence links it to the theme of the paragraph or section. The theme of a sentence is located at the start and establishes the focus of the sentence – what it is about. This is followed by new information on that theme – the point of the sentence. The points of each sentence add up to make the point of the paragraph. For example, look at the following initial sentences from the first two sections of Extract 2.4.

Theme	Point
I ...	work for a charity called Youth Clubs North.
The Outdoor Centre, which is called Caxton House, ...	is based in Kendal.

In each case, the theme of the sentence relates to the theme of the paragraph. The first locates the writer in the context of his workplace and the work; the second describes the physical aspects of the workplace.

The theme is the part of the sentence which comes before the main verb. It can vary considerably in length, for example:

Theme	Point
Thrift Bank	began as a tiny Belfast banking company called the Thrift Banking Partnership.
Following a takeover in the late eighties, these	outlets were renamed National Thrift Bank.

The choice of theme at the start of each sentence affects the impression given by the text and how it fits together.

Activity 2.3

Purpose: to identify the themes in two texts and the effect they have on the reader.

Task: reread Extracts 2.3 and 2.4. In a table with the headings below, list the themes of each sentence. In some sentences the themes have more than one component; in others they are very simple. The themes of the first two sentences in each text are given to get you started.

Extract 2.3	Extract 2.4
Thrift Bank	I ...
From the very beginning Thrift	The main aim of the charity

Compare your answers with those suggested in the Answer section.

Comment

The list of themes shows that Extract 2.3 focuses on the bank itself, as nearly every sentence begins with a word or phrase referring to it, often preceded by a time-related phrase such as *In 1840 ...*, or *Following a takeover in the late eighties ...* This focuses the reader's attention on the bank and its history in a chronological order, the sentences being linked by these two themes.

In Extract 2.4 there is more variety of themes, including *The Outdoor Centre ...*, *The residential side of the organisation ...*, *The success of the Centre ...*, *This understanding ....* This shows a different approach to the topic, the range of themes focusing the reader's attention on different aspects of the organisation.

How sentences are linked by themes and points

In Extract 2.3, the sentences are linked by references to the bank, and by references to time which follow in sequence. In Extract 2.4, where the themes vary from sentence to sentence, how are the sentences connected? If you look closely you should see that in each sentence there is an element, usually in the theme, which links it to what has gone before. For example:

Theme	Point
I ...	work for **a charity** called Youth Clubs North.
The main aim of **the charity**	is to aid young people throughout northern England.
This	is done primarily through the provision of outdoor education in a residential setting.

The word *charity*, which is part of the point of the first sentence, telling you where the writer (theme) works, occurs as part of the theme of the second sentence. In the third sentence the word *This*, referring to *to aid young people*, links the theme of the third sentence to the second.

Activity2.4 ....

Purpose: to identify theme structure and judge its effect.

Task: Extracts 2.5 and 2.6 in Resource Book 3 are two more examples of students describing their work environment. The extracts appear twice, once in their original format and then as a table.

Read the extracts in the tables and underline the theme in each sentence. Then make a note in the right-hand column of what links the theme to what went before in the text. The first four sentences in Extract 2.5 are done for you as an example.

Compare your answers with those suggested in the Answer section.

Comment ....

The choice of theme and point in each sentence conveys information about how the writer perceives the information being given and how they want the reader to perceive it. It gives an idea of which aspects of the topic are most important for the writer so that, in Extract 2.5, Mr Li, the owner of the company being described, is clearly considered to be a key figure, since he is referred to in the themes of four out of the nine sentences. In Extract 2.6, most sentences have a theme expressing a time factor, such as *In its formative years in the 1940s, it ...*, or *With the development of e-commerce, the Electric Town ...*, together with a reference to the Akihabara Electric Town, making it similar to Extract 2.3, where the development of the Thrift Bank is described over time.

The theme of the first sentence in a text may convey new information, although it is probably referred to in a title or a heading, so that the reader is aware of it before starting to read. The development of the direction of the text is made clear by making sure that the theme of every following sentence links in some way to the information which was given before. This enables the reader to follow the flow of information easily, although sometimes a new theme is introduced which is not linked to the previous one.

Having examined in some detail these examples of other students' information-giving writing, you now need to think about the organisation you will describe. Imagine what information you would need to give your fellow students and your tutor in order for them to have an idea of the organisation you work in and the different factors that impact on your working environment. Each writer you have looked at so far has also raised an issue facing their company at present. If you are not employed outside the home, your home environment and the tasks you have to achieve there could be the subject of this first very brief report. Alternatively, you could describe a previous situation which you have worked in, a family business or a company you have studied online.

Activity 2.5 ....

Purpose: to produce a short text describing your work environment.

Task: return to the task described in Section 2.1 and focus at this stage on writing:

a description of your organisation in its environment, and the issues that are important to it at the present time.

The best way to start is probably to brainstorm the situation you have chosen to describe, noting down all the aspects that you think might be relevant to give your readers a clear picture of the situation. You might use a key concept map for doing this. Decide whether you want to discuss either the development of the organisation or a particular problem existing now. Now write a short text describing the development of the organisation, or a particular problem existing now.

There is no answer for this activity because it is personal to you.

Comment ....

When you have written something it is a good idea to set it aside for a day and then return to it with fresh eyes. At that point you will be better able to judge the impression your writing conveys.

2.4 Functions of a report (2): analysing

This section moves on from the descriptive part of the report to the part which is analytical. In Extract 2.4, the writer mentions a model which is a useful tool for evaluating development plans: the SMART (Specific, Measurable, Achievable, Realistic and Time-related) model. This model is especially useful for organising texts because it provides a means of processing information through the use of ready-made headings under which to group information. You saw another example of this in the Good Days Out report in Session 1, where the 'consumer decision-making process' model was used.

Models give a framework which can help in the analysis of a situation. But they need to be seen as tools from which to choose. Writers and readers both need to be aware that the choice of model will influence the outcome of the analysis. This is a consequence of the structure devised in the model but also of the terminology used to put ideas into categories. It is discussed below using the example of a SWOT analysis.

The SWOT model

The writer of Text 2.2 in Resource Book 3 chose the SWOT (Strengths, Weaknesses, Opportunities and Threats) model to analyse his organisation in its environment. This model, which was introduced in Book 1, can be applied to almost any situation since aspects of the four categories (SWOT) can usually be perceived in any context. As you will recall, this model involves creating a table containing four boxes labelled Strengths, Weaknesses, Opportunities and Threats. The organisation is considered under these headings, and information is added to each box as appropriate.

Note in the above example that certain items listed under weaknesses and threats could, depending on the analyst's perception, be considered strengths or opportunities. For example, 'staff having to multi-task', in the weaknesses box, could be considered a strength. There may also be factors which could be placed in more than one box depending on the circumstances, such as 'government policies', which could constitute threats or opportunities depending on the policy. Nevertheless, this model provides a useful tool to start analysing any given situation. How useful do you think the SWOT model would be in analysing your current working environment?

Some other models

Other models are more specific in their terminology. The STEEP model, introduced in Book 1, looks at Social, Technological, Economic, Environmental and Political factors in assessing future trends and possibilities. Similar models are: PEST, which analyses Political, Economic, Social and Technological factors; PESTLE, which adds Legal and Environmental to PEST; and the stakeholder model, which was introduced in Book 1. The headings used in these models are more neutral than those of the SWOT analysis.

The PESTLE model

In the next activity you will look at an example of the PESTLE model applied by a student to the organisation and environment of a police force.

Activity 2.6 ....

Purpose: to consider the terminology used in the model and your understanding of the terms used.

Task 1: create a table with the headings below. Find a dictionary definition of each key concept in the left-hand column and write the definition in the middle column. Then, in the right-hand column, write your understanding of what each term means and which aspects of the situation it might include.

PEST = Political, Economis, Social Technological

PESTLE   Nt   + Legal, Envirnmental

Key concept	Dictionary definition	Your understanding
Political		
Economic		
Social		
Technological		
Legal		
Environmental		

Compare your answers with those suggested in the Answer section.

Task 2: read Extract 2.7 in Resource Book 3 and consider how each term has been interpreted. For example, the term 'political' is interpreted in the sense of 'party political'. Are there other ways of using this term? What does it mean to you? What would it mean in business if you said 'It was a political decision'?

The answer to this task is discussed in the comment below.

Comment

If you used table headings to consider your local police force, would you have thought of the same factors? The writer interprets 'political' in a fairly narrow sense, related to the party in power. She could also have extended her analysis more broadly under the headings 'Economic' and 'Environmental'. Models are useful tools for analysis; they also provide a terminology which can be used to help a report writer give a clear picture of a scenario. However, most terms have more than one meaning and their use can be interpreted in different ways. Ideas stimulated by the model need to be developed further in writing and alternative perspectives should be considered. A diagram should always be followed by an explanation giving the writer's interpretation of the information represented. An example of how a student used another model is described next.

Porter's Five Forces Model

This model is designed to enable businesses to identify the competitive pressures they may be facing. The key concepts Porter uses are: *established competitors, new entrants to the market, substitute products, the bargaining power of suppliers* and *the bargaining power of customers*. In Text 2.1 in Resource Book 3 there is an example of how one student applied this model to inform her description of her organisation and its environment.

Activity 2.7

Purpose: to recognise the role of a model in the writer's analysis of her organisation and its environment.

Task 1: look at the diagram of Porter's Five Forces Model in Text 2.1, in the section 'Description of my organisation'. Then read the student's analysis. Create a table with the headings below and list the concepts from the model that the student used in her analysis.

Concept word(s) used	Number of times used	Meaning of the word(s)

Compare your answers with those suggested in the Answer section.

Task 2: now consider the following questions.
- Have all the concepts been used?
- Are those included used appropriately?
- Are there reasons why this is a good model to describe a banking environment?
- Are there reasons why it is not?

Comment

The writer identifies *Industry Competitors* and *Substitutes* in relation to her organisation; however, she has not added any information under the headings *Suppliers* and *Buyers*. This is possibly because the model is better applied to a manufacturing or a retail company and the concept of suppliers is not relevant to banks.

In the next activity you consider the first paragraph of the student's analysis and consider how it is structured and how it relates to the model. The aim is to understand how a model can determine how the themes of paragraphs and sentences are chosen and how these link back to both the model and each other. They are interconnected throughout and the paragraph is an essential complement to any diagrammatic explanation.

Activity 2.8

Purpose: to look at how the written analysis and the model are linked.

Task: look at the second paragraph of the explanation.

Identify the **theme** and the **point** in each sentence and state where the writer has made **links** between a sentence and the Five Forces Model either by using words from the model or by explicit reference to the model. The first sentence is done for you as an example.

Sentence no.	Theme	Point	Link to model
1	Being a member of staff in a financial sector	allows me to identify with all of the above five types	The above five types
2			
3			
4			
5			
6			

Compare your answers with those suggested in the Answer section.

Comment ....

The writer uses Porter's framework to examine her working environment, adding information about competitors and substitutes in her sector. Without her written analysis, the diagram would not be very informative, yet it has served the purpose of structuring her thoughts and giving her the stimulus to elaborate on them. It has given her concepts and terminology to use in her analysis. In this paragraph some of the sentences are linked not only to each other but also to an outside entity, the model. Some do not link specifically to the model but only to previous sentences in the text.

In choosing a model, the categories that the model establishes need to be considered carefully for applicability to the particular organisation being analysed and the purpose of the analysis. As you saw, in a bank, the category of supplier is not relevant. In other organisations the relevance may vary: for example, in a school or other educational establishment there will be some suppliers but they are not central to the organisation's activity; whereas in the clothing industry supply is of central importance.

Different models have been devised for different purposes as shown in Table 2.1.

Table 2.1 Purposes of models

Model	Purpose
SWOT	Used to analyse the current situation of an organisation. Helpful in a situation where a review is being contemplated or arguments put forward for change
Porter's Five Forces	Used to identify the competitive pressures in an organisation's near environment and gain understanding of a particular sector of industry
PESTLE or STEEP	Used to scan the broader environment and the position of an organisation within it
Stakeholder analysis	Used to assess the interests of the various stakeholders in an organisation so that the organisation can decide how to meet their needs

In analysing your organisation, think first about the aims and objectives of the report, then the issues that are important to the organisation (which you considered in the previous section), before deciding on a model. You should also refer back to the SWOT analysis you did in Activity 2.6 and the examples of the application of models in this session.

Activity 2.9 ....

Purpose: to apply a model to analyse your organisation and its environment.

Task: use one of the models discussed above to produce a short text analysing your work environment.

Select from the models the one you think would be most useful in analysing your working environment, considering the terminology used and how appropriate it is for your purpose. Choose a model that you think will help you to understand the factors in the environment which impact on your work and will also make it possible for you to explain this clearly to others.

Now use your chosen model to draw a diagram representing your organisation's current situation. Then write an analysis (300–400 words) elaborating on the information that appears on your diagram, using the terminology from the diagram. This piece of writing will form part of your final activity for this session.

There is no answer for this activity because it is personal to you.

Comment

If you chose appropriately, the model should have helped you to understand the factors in the environment that impinge on your organisation and enabled you to report them to others. You might want to return to this piece of writing later and change it. It can also be included in the report you produce at the end of this session.

2.5 Functions of a report (3): explaining and justifying

In Section 2.4 you looked at models for analysis. To carry out analysis, you must have data (or facts about the situation) to analyse. In Book 1, these data, or facts, were referred to as the details and examples which provide the basis for the high-level generalisations in the analysis. In Book 2, data were referred to as the basis for the explanation and the claims in an argument. In this section, data – particularly data in diagrams – are examined more closely.

> **Definition**
>
> The word 'data' comes from the Latin meaning 'given' and is used to mean facts or information. Strictly speaking, it is a plural noun, so we say, for example, 'The data <u>are</u> convincing'. However, it is often used as a singular noun, 'The data <u>is</u> convincing'.

Because of the requirement for clarity, visual representations of data are commonly used in reports. One reason is because much information can be represented very succinctly, saving space and the reader's time. Another reason is that visual representations can be very convincing. It is important to remember that the way in which data are presented carries information about how the writer wants the data to be understood, and affects the readers' understanding. For example, the differences in intervals on the vertical axes of Figures 2.1 and 2.2 give a very different impression of how the number of staff has changed in Years 1–6. Also, in Figure 2.1, the effect of beginning from zero has been to compress the data shown on the vertical axis and so make it harder to understand the graph. In Figure 2.2, the vertical scale begins at 200 and the scale has been extended so that the information presented in the graph is much clearer.

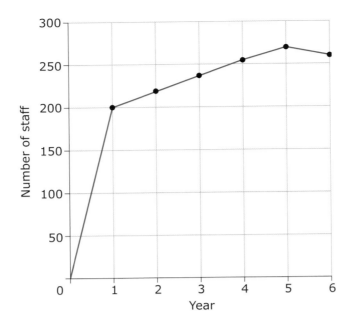

Figure 2.1 Number of staff in Years 1–6 (compressed)

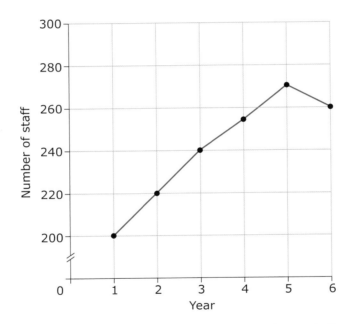

Figure 2.2 Number of staff in Years 1–6 (extended)

Writers may choose to draw on data collected by other people (**secondary sources**) or they may have collected their own data (**primary source**) and, therefore, be creating their own visual representations.

Using representations of data from secondary sources

This part of Session 2 focuses particularly on Sections A and B of the Influential Document Checklist. You might find it useful to look at the checklist in the Appendix before carrying on.

Many reports incorporate data collected from a range of secondary sources. The main points to bear in mind here are, first, that the source should be one that the intended readers will recognise as reliable, so that the data are credible, and, second, that the data are represented in a way that adds clarification and weight to the points the report writer is seeking to clarify and/or justify. Book 2, Section 2.5 gives some indicators of how to select source materials which are appropriate for academic writing. It also discusses the issue of bias in materials, which needs to be taken into consideration when using any source. However reputable a source, it will not be free from an element of bias, and writers should always demonstrate their awareness of this.

Sources which may be considered reliable include:

- government ministries and organisations (these are more reliable in some countries than in others)
- international organisations such as the World Bank, the European Union, the International Monetary Fund and the International Labour Organisation
- well-known companies such as Nike and Wal-Mart
- non-governmental organisations (NGOs) such as Friends of the Earth and Fair Trade
- academic sources such as books, refereed journals and unpublished theses.

(**Note:** when you use the internet, sites with *.gov*, *.org* or *.ac* in their address are generally considered fairly reliable.)

When using secondary sources, you should always give clear and full references so that the reader can check the source of the data and decide whether the writer has used them appropriately.

Visual representations include a range of ways of presenting information. If you use secondary data, the person or organisation which produced the data will have chosen how to represent them. Your task is to understand, interpret and possibly question this data, and to highlight the information relevant to your purpose.

Writing about visual representations

Academic convention requires that all visual representations are accompanied by a written explanation. This is important because visuals nearly always contain more information than is needed to make the point, so the writer must select which information they want the reader to focus on. The written explanation points out and highlights aspects of the data, sets these in context and provides a comment from the writer.

You have already seen in Activities 2.7 and 2.8 how a student's paragraph explaining her use of a model to describe her organisation complemented the information given in the diagram. The same applies to all visual representations of data. They need to relate to the topic being addressed.

The point of commenting on data is for the writer to make clear their position about the information that is given, including their reasons for choosing it and/or representing it in a particular way.

Commentaries therefore generally start by introducing a theme which informs the reader of what the commentary is about. Data are then selected from the representation to focus on this theme and justify it. These refer directly to the information in the chart and generally use phrases such as:

As can be seen from ...

According to ...

As shown in ...

It can be seen in ...

The writer may also choose to compare different aspects of the data using phrases such as:

In relation to .....

Compared with ....

Double that of ...

Twice that of ...

Half that of ...

In these types of sentence the statements are often approximations of the information in the diagram rather than precise descriptions. They also serve the writer's purpose in justifying their commentary.

Expressions which are used to indicate changes that are usually represented by graphs include particular nouns, often qualified by adjectives, for example:

Adjective	Noun
Minimal	Rise
Marked	Increase
Dramatic	Decline
Steep	Fluctuation

Other words specifically associated with graphs, such as: *trend, curve, peak, plateau* and *trough* are also used.

The writer will choose which aspects of the data to highlight to achieve the aim of the commentary. The final sentence summarises what the writer intends the reader to understand from the data and the commentary combined.

Activity 2.10

Purpose: to look at an example of how a writer has discussed a visual in a report.

Task: read Extract 2.8 and then look at Table 2.2 below. Pick out the sentences in the extract in which the writer carries out the actions listed below the table. Write them in the space beside the correct action.

Table 2.2 Kazakhstan market summary, 1999–2003

	1999	*2000*	*2001*	*2002*	*2003*
Population (m)	14.9	14.8	14.8	14.8	14.8
GDP (US$ billion at market exchange rates)	16.9	18.3	21.5	23.8	28.0
GDP growth (%)	2.7	9.8	12.2	9.5	9.1
GDP per capita (US$)	1133	1231	1450	1600	1820

(Source: The Banker, 2002)

Action	Sentence
Introduces the theme of the paragraph	
Gives exact information from the chart	
Gives approximate information from the chart	
Gives information not included in the chart	
Gives his own view on the data	
Makes a concluding statement	

Compare your answers with those suggested in the Answer section.

Comment ....

The writer introduces the topic very briefly with a general statement about the economy of Kazakhstan, then selects particular data from the chart and adds his perspective, which can be deduced from expressions such as *Remarkably* ... and *which is unprecedented*. He adds information to that contained in the chart as well as repeating some of it, and gives his own comment at the end which expresses his overall view of the situation.

The next visual representation you are asked to look at gives information in the form of a pie chart (Figure 2.3). The writer has again started with a statement which gives the theme of the paragraph. She has then selected information from the pie chart in order to build an argument for her concluding statement.

Activity 2.11 ....

Purpose: to examine the structure of a commentary on a visual representation.

Task: look at the pie chart in Extract 2.9 and the accompanying commentary. Then in the version of Extract 2.9 in the table below, write the purpose of each sentence on the right-hand side. For your convenience the pie chart is also shown here in Figure 2.3.

Sentence in the commentary	Purpose of sentence
With the development of construction in Beijing and the increase in people's income, many investors are attracted to Beijing, especially to the real estate market because that has become the fastest improving industry.	
According to the Beijing Statistics Committee, in the first quarter of 2002 there were 1024 new foreign investors approved by government and out of a total investment of 2 billion US dollars, 0.4 billion was invested in the real estate market.	
As can be seen from the chart, many businesses in Japan and Hong Kong invest in the real estate market in Beijing.	
This is because of the state of the economies in their countries, and the belief that the price of real estate in Beijing will keep on rising until the 2008 Olympic games.	
Nevertheless the chart shows that by far the largest proportion of investment in the Beijing real estate market comes from North and Latin America, with more than twice the proportion invested by Europe.	
According to the chart, Chinese investors are only accountable for three-quarters as much as Europeans.	
These figures suggest a possibly dangerous over-reliance on overseas investment in real estate in Beijing.	

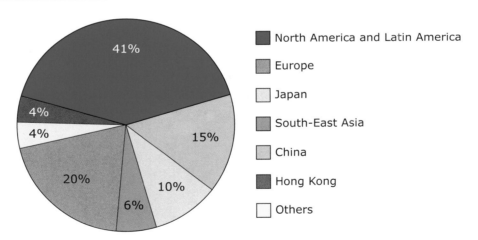

Figure 2.3 Investors in Beijing real-estate market by countries and regions

Compare your answers with those suggested in the Answer section.

Comment ....

The writer suggests in her conclusion that the amount of foreign investment in real estate in Beijing could have a negative side. Starting with a general statement, she then uses information from another source as well as selecting factual information from the chart to give evidence for her argument, adding her own explanation for some of the data. Her descriptions of data from the chart are not exact and she adds her own detail to make her point. For example, she says *by far the largest proportion of investment ...* This reinforces her negative conclusion which describes a *dangerous over-reliance*. In this way, she gives her own interpretation of the data. The process is similar to building an argument in an essay, which you studied in Book 2.

In writing about your organisation and its environment, you should consider whether you have data which could be represented graphically in a way that would make your report more accessible to the reader, either in the form of statistics and figures or in terms of representing ideas diagrammatically.

However, as discussed above, as well as the connection between the writing and the visual, there is a structure within each text which connects the sentences and paragraphs. In this session you have met again the idea of **theme** and **point** in paragraphs and sentences. These organise a text to make it easy to understand. Session 3 in Book 2 introduced the ways in which information in sentences is linked and connected with information in other sentences.

Putting your report together

The difficult part of structuring a report is deciding how to divide the information you are presenting in the most effective way. In Text 2.1 the writer has structured her report under 'Background', 'Work Roles', 'Description of My Organisation' and 'The Purpose of My Organisation's Mission or Vision Statement'. Text 2.2 sticks more closely to the title in using 'The Organisation in the Environment' as a heading but it also uses 'The Operations Director's Role'. In your report you should start with the heading 'Introduction' as the writer does, and end with a section under the heading 'Conclusion', as Text 2.1 does. However, it is up to you to choose the headings in between, based on the themes of the paragraphs you want to include.

So far in this session you have drafted paragraphs as you worked through the activities. Now you need to consider the order in which to integrate them in your report, what headings to give them and whether any changes need to be made, or information added or taken away. In doing this, you need to consider what message you want to convey to your reader.

Activity 2.12   ....

Purpose: to structure your report, give headings to sections and decide what needs to be added.

Task: list the sections which will make up your report on 'My Organisation in Its Environment', bearing in mind that it should be no more than 800 words long and include the texts you have produced so far in this session. Make a note of what you need to do to complete the report. Consider the overall impression you want to make on the reader.

Comment ....

You will have reread the texts you have written so far and thought about what you would like to say to conclude your report. You will also have considered how to introduce it, how to link the various sections and what headings you will give them.

Conclusion

The conclusion is arguably the most important section of a report. Readers who are in a hurry may go straight to the conclusion, particularly if the report does not include recommendations, because they will want an overview of the subject and to find out what the writer thinks. It is a good idea to have your conclusion clear in your head before you finalise the structure of the report so that you can build up to it effectively. The conclusion should summarise briefly the main points that have been made and state clearly what conclusion the writer draws from them. Text 2.10 in Resource Book 3 is an example of a possible conclusion to a report like the one you are writing.

Introduction

Generally, it is easiest to write the introduction after the rest of the report has been put together. This is because in the introduction the writer explains to the reader what is covered in the report, why it was written and what its aims are. It should be brief and to the point. Text 2.11 in Resource Book 3 is an example of such an introduction.

Activity 2.13 ....

Purpose: to put together previously drafted paragraphs, edit and add any necessary components to create a short, coherent report.

Task: reread the paragraphs you wrote for Activities 2.5, 2.6, 2.9 and 2.12. Write a conclusion and an introduction. You could adapt the paragraph you wrote for Activity 2.5 as an introduction. Do any necessary editing and add any recommendations, appendices, bibliography or references and glossary you consider necessary. After you have read the comment below, do the assignment activity at the end of this section.

Comment ....

Your report should now read as a coherent whole. To make sure, put it aside for at least 24 hours (longer if possible), then reread it and make any changes you think would improve it.

Assignment activity

Send your draft report to your tutor for feedback. When you receive the feedback, produce another draft of the report, using the feedback to guide you, and save both drafts of the report for the assessment at the end of this book.

2.6 Conclusion

This session was concerned with the mechanics of drafting a short academic report. It focused on the language used in reports, in particular how the flow of information can be managed through the concepts of **theme** and **point** in order to make writing clear and easy to read. It examined how visual representations can be used to clarify thoughts and information and improve communication. The session also revisited the characteristics and possible structures of a report, as discussed in Session 1. Through the session, you produced a short report about your organization, its environment and your role within it.

2.7 Review

In this session you should have:

- applied what you learned in Session 1 about the general characteristics of reports
- examined three different functions of report writing – informing, analysing and justifying
- analysed different ways of using grammar to manage information flow
- looked at ways of representing information diagrammatically in reports
- discussed aspects of report writing online with fellow students
- written a short academic report.

2.8 Answer section

Activity 2.1

Task 1

Section	Text 2.1	Text 2.2
Table of contents	✓	✗
Introduction	✗	✓
Discussion under numbered and/or headed sections	✓	✓
Conclusion	✓	✗
Recommendations	✗	✗
References	✗	✓
Appendices	✗	✗

Activity 2.2

Although both texts are essentially giving information, the information is of different kinds. In Extract 2.3 the information is the sort you could find on the bank's website or in publicity materials. It mainly gives historical facts. The information could be addressed to potential customers or investors. Extract 2.4 seems to be addressed to readers who might have a role in changing how the business operates. The writer clearly feels that changes need to be made in the organisation. His comment, *very little strategic management has taken place,* indicates that he sees room for improvement and he goes on to say, *In order to improve ...,* and later, *hopefully the organisation can grow and become more efficient and effective.* This makes Extract 2.4 more evaluative whereas Extract 2.3 is more factual, focusing on the bank as part of a successful organisation and on giving positive information to the reader, for example *Thrift remains the bank of choice for the majority of businesses ...* Both extracts are written in formal style.

Activity 2.3

Extract 2.3	Extract 2.4
Thrift Bank	I
From the very beginning Thrift	The main aim of the charity
Throughout its history, the Bank's fortunes	This
In 1840, the Bank	The Outdoor Centre which is called Caxton House Outdoor Centre
Following a takeover in the late eighties, these outlets	This
Today, Thrift	The residential side of the organization
There	Throughout that time very little strategic management
A world-wide network of sister banks	
Thrift	The success of the Centre
The changeover	In order to improve the ways in which Caxton House operates it
	This understanding
	Through SMART strategic objectives hopefully the organisation

Activity 2.4

Extract 2.5

Text	Notes on how theme links back
Liaoning Decoration and Engineering Co. Ltd was founded in 1995.	Theme of the paragraph
It is a typical SME that employs about 89 staff and with registered capital of about US$3 million.	'It' refers to Liaoning Decoration and Engineering Co. Ltd, the first theme
Mr Li, the owner of this company, graduate of Shenyang University, senior construction engineer, is an expert in the construction industry.	'Mr Li' is a new theme but 'this company' refers to the above.
This company was set up at the time of reform and open policy in China's economy.	As above
At that time, construction in Liaoning province was flourishing, so that with the encouraging policy from the local government, and the limitations of the competitors, this company got the first bucket of gold quickly.	'At that time' refers to 1995, the point of the first sentence, 'construction' refers to information in the point of the third sentence.
Meanwhile Mr Li noticed the lack of excellent import commodities from advanced western countries which attracted the Chinese consumer, and in the construction industry, there were fewer people dealing with high quality and well-designed ceramic products for family use.	Refers to theme of third sentence.
Mr Li recognised that this is a rather rare chance for himself which would stimulate the development of his business.	As above
Therefore, without further inspection of the real market, he decided to invest all his funds in this item.	'He' refers to Mr Li, as above.
However, as a result of sales problems, there was a big amount of capital restricted by this investment, thus, flow capital and the suitable market has become a pressing issue to solve.	New theme

Extract 2.6

Text	Notes on how theme links back
The Akihabara Electrical Town Association self-describes the Akihabara Electric Town as the world's biggest Electrical Equipment Town, with a collection of about 250 electronics stores (from mega-stores to tiny parts suppliers) concentrated within it, near the Akihabara Station in Central Tokyo.	Theme of the paragraph
This may be true, since there are no comparable concentrations of electrical shops elsewhere in the world.	'This' refers to the Electric Town's self-description in the first sentence.
In its formative years in the 1940s, it was a sort-of black market for selling radios and radio parts for the domestic market.	'Its' refers to Akihabara Electric Town.
Over the years, as many of the leading Japanese Electronics Companies began using Akihabara as the place to test-launch their latest products, it developed into the place-to-go for electronics enthusiasts and it began to attract enthusiasts from abroad.	'It' refers to Akihabara.
As the number of overseas visitors increased, many mega stores catering specifically to the needs of tourists have been opened, including duty free purchase options.	'Many mega stores' refers to Akihabara.
Actually, apart from die-hard enthusiasts, the Electric Town is not well known outside of Japan.	'The Electric Town' is as above.
With the development of e-commerce, the Electric Town is beginning to lose some of its uniqueness and competitiveness as the place-to-go to find the best electronics products.	As above
The Akihabara Electrical Town Association and the Tokyo Metropolitan Government are collaborating to market the Electric Town more aggressively.	As above

Activity 2.6

Key concept	Dictionary definition	Your understanding
Political	of or relating to the state, government, the body politic, public administration, policy making, **but also** relating to the parties and the partisan aspects of politics	Can mean party political, or more generally related to government and the state
Economic	Of or relating to an economy, economics or finance, **but also** concerning or affecting material resources or welfare	Used in different ways to refer to finance, affordability or policy on finance
Social	Denoting or relating to human society or any of its subdivisions, **but also** relating to communal activities	Very broad meaning covering most aspects of human life
Technological	Relating to the application of practical sciences to industry or commerce **and** the methods, theory and practices governing such application	Specifically about practical, material factors to do with infrastructure and equipment
Legal	Lawful, of or relating to law, **but also** recognised, enforceable or having a remedy at law	Fairly clear meaning but needs to be distinguished from 'moral' and 'acceptable'
Environmental	Relating to the external conditions or surroundings in which people live or work	More general than the sense in which it is often used relating to nature

(Source: all definitions are from *Collins English Dictionary*, 21st Century Edition, 2000)

Activity 2.7

Task 1

Concept word(s) used	Number of times used	Meaning of the word(s)
five types	1	The kinds of pressure on companies identified by Porter
(established) competitors	4	Rival firms which have been around for a long time
threat	2	Factor which may be a danger to the success of a company
substitutes	3	Other providers which offer the same goods or services
suppliers	1	Organisations which supply goods to companies

Activity 2.8

Sentence no.	Theme	Point	Link to model
1	Being a member of staff in a financial sector	allows me to identify with all of the above five types	the above five types
2	In the town in which I work there	are five different Building Societies and two other established competitors (Bank of Ireland and Ulster Bank) which are all seen as a threat to our service.	established competitors threat
3	As mentioned previously 'Thrift'	has been bought out by a Dutch company called 'Utrecht Bank'.	–
4	In Holland, Utrecht Bank	is an old, distinguished and select bank – a market leader and a strong commercial bank that also attracts affluent retail customers.	–
5	The changeover	will occur at Easter 2006 and will involve all employees going on new training and slight changes occurring to our logo (but not many as Thrift does not want people to think it is a different business altogether).	–
6	This type of banking	will be a threat to other financial providers throughout Northern Ireland	threat

Activity 2.10

Action	Sentence
Introduces the theme of the paragraph	The current economic growth in Kazakhstan started in mid 1999
Gives exact information from the chart	As can be seen from Table 1, GDP at current exchange rates has almost doubled from £16.9 billion in 1999 to £28 billion in 2003
Gives approximate information from the chart	The decline in population has stopped at a level of 14.8 million people
Gives information not included in the chart	The government target for 2002 was the GDP growth of 7.0%. However, it was easily exceeded ...
Gives his own view on the data	... living standards have significantly improved with GDP per capita raised from $1133 in 1999 to $1820 in 2003. Remarkably the real change in GDP even reached the double digit growth of 12.2% in 2003.
Makes a concluding statement	Economic growth and low rate of inflation have significantly reduced the risks.

Activity 2.11

Sentence in the commentary	Purpose of sentence
With the development of construction in Beijing and the increase in people's income, many investors are attracted to Beijing, especially to the real estate market because that has become the fastest improving industry.	Introduces the writer's theme
According to the Beijing Statistics Committee, in the first quarter of 2002 there were 1024 new foreign investors approved by government and out of a total investment of 2 billion US dollars, 0.4 billion was invested in the real estate market.	Provides evidence from an official source (but not included in the chart)
As can be seen from the chart, many businesses in Japan and Hong Kong invest in the real estate market in Beijing.	Reinforces theme and previous evidence with information from chart
This is because of the state of the economies in their countries, and the belief that the price of real estate in Beijing will keep on rising until the 2008 Olympic games.	Gives her own explanation of the phenomenon shown in the chart
Nevertheless the chart shows that by far the largest proportion of investment in the Beijing real estate market comes from North and Latin America, with more than twice the proportion invested by Europe.	Uses an approximation of information from the chart to justify her conclusion
According to the chart, Chinese investors are only accountable for three-quarters as much as Europeans.	As above
These figures suggest a possibly dangerous over-reliance on overseas investment in real estate in Beijing.	Expresses her conclusion

SESSION **3 Self-evaluation documents**

3.1 Introduction

In this session, you will read and write performance-evaluation reports. There are three situations in which such texts are produced. On business studies courses, students are asked to write skills-audit reports to record their development during the course. When applying for jobs, applicants write a personal statement supporting their application. In the workplace, appraisal reports are a part of continuing professional development and performance management.

Performance is a concept that can be related to both organisational and individual activity. The concept map in Figure 3.1 shows these two aspects of performance. The report you wrote on 'My Organisation in Its Environment' in Session 2 was concerned mostly with organisational performance. The focus in this session is on *individual performance*, and is therefore related to the larger field of human resource management.

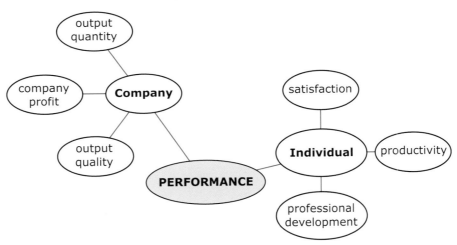

Figure 3.1   Mind map showing individual and organisational performance criteria

There are similarities in the way the two types of performance are discussed. But there is a significant difference which will be the main focus of this session. Individual performance is **personal**. This raises questions about what writing style to use for communicating about it.

Much of the communication in this course has tended towards the more impersonal and objective style of writing. However, there have been some exceptions. In the customer decision-making process text about Good Days Out (Session 1), a less academic style was used to communicate with a non-specialist workplace audience. In 'My Organisation in Its Environment', a more personal style was possible in response to the topic of *my* organisation.

Writing may become **more personal** for two reasons:

1   the audience is less formal and the writer wants a more personal kind of relationship with them
2   the subject matter the writer is dealing with is their personal experience.

The second reason is particularly relevant to writing in business studies where you are expected to connect academic study to your personal experience of business.

Writing in a more or less personal style sometimes relates to the idea of a writer's **voice**. Voice is the 'sound' of a text. It is the writer's personality coming through in the words of the text. This can be difficult for some people when writing formal text.

If you want to see an example of different voices in writing, look again at the two economics texts from Session 1 (Texts 1.10 and 1.11 in Resource Book 3). The two banks are communicating different personalities to their customers: one uses a personal and involved voice; the other has a more formal and distant voice.

In this session, you will focus on *skills-audit reports* from business studies courses.

The skills-audit reports in this session are probably the most personal kind of university or workplace text. This session will concentrate on how to write such texts so that they are both personal and professional at the same time.

Learning outcomes

In this session you will:

* develop your understanding of how skills audits are structured for their audience and purpose
* develop the language of evaluation used in skills audits
* develop skills in using your personal experience, in both academic writing and as the basis for self evaluation
* learn more about the use of formal and informal, personal and impersonal language in documents.

3.2 Skills audits

Skills audits are a common kind of business studies text. They are usually written by students on business studies courses to reflect on the skills they currently have, report on the skills they have developed, or plan the development of their skills in the future. In this course, you have written reflections while studying case study analysis and essay writing.

In this session you will look more closely at what is involved in writing this kind of reflection text and produce a final text of your own. To start this process, do the following SWOT analysis on yourself.

Activity 3.1   ....

Purpose: to gather information for a self-reflection report.

Task: Text 3.1 in Resource Book 3 shows two sets of skills which this course was designed to develop. Read through the list of skills. Then create two tables with the headings below. Write reflection notes in the two columns. Use any records or reflection texts you have written since the beginning of the course to help you. Refer to the skills lists in Text 3.1.

My strengths at the beginning of this course	*My weaknesses at the beginning of this course*
My strengths now	*My weaknesses now*

When you have finished, save your tables in MyStuff on the course website. You will need them later in this session.

There are no suggested answers for this activity because it is personal to you.

Next you will do some activities where you look at several self-evaluation reports written by other students. This gives you the opportunity to reflect on how these reports are written. In the process, you will read other students' views about developing communication skills, learn to judge the effectiveness of some self-evaluation reports, and develop additional skills and knowledge to use in writing a self-evaluation report of your own.

3.3 Personal experience in business studies

Because this session is particularly concerned with the **personal** in business studies, the first skills-evaluation report you will read is a student's evaluation of her skill in using personal experience in business studies writing.

This section begins with three activities which explore how you do this. You will first reflect on your own personal experience and then you will read the report by another student.

Activity 3.2 ···

Purpose: to prepare a short piece of personal writing.

Task: write a description of a job you have had. It can be a full-time, part-time, paid or unpaid job. If you have not had a formal job outside the home, write about a job you do in the home. Imagine you are writing this for someone who is thinking about taking up the same kind of job and has written asking you to give them some idea about it. There are no further instructions about what you should include in your description at this stage. The decision is yours. Write at least a page – or more if you like. Write the text in a style that feels natural to you. Use paragraphs and paragraph theme sentences to organise the text. Pay attention to sentence links and connections. As you will post this text on the online course forum, you may want to redraft it.

There is no answer for this activity but it is discussed in the comment below.

Comment ···

The context and purpose of this text was left open, to give you as much freedom as possible to decide on the content, organisation and style you used. It is quite unnatural to write with so little context and purpose, so you may think your text is not very natural. However, even without a clear context and purpose, you will have made decisions about what to include, how to organise the text, and what style of language to use.

You will now consider how the personal experience you have written about can be framed, using business studies course material.

This business studies material comes from the Open University course, B120 *An introduction to business studies*. This extract is from Book 2, *An Introduction to Human Resource Management in Business*, Section 2, 'Designing satisfying work'. As this is from the Course Guide and not the Course Reader, the organisation and language style of the text (the voice) is not as academic as it is in the Reader. The extract presents a business model known as the *job characteristics model*. First, you will read the extract and identify what concepts make up the model. Then you will use these concepts to frame the personal experience of a job you have just written about.

Activity 3.3

Purpose: to study the job characteristics model in order to apply it to personal job experience.

Task: read Extract 3.2 in Resource Book 3 and summarise the main features of the job characteristics model. Do this by filling in the gaps in Figure 3.2 below. The first concept is done as an example.

There is no answer for this activity. If you would like to check your understanding of the extract, exchange your answers with the students you worked with in Online Activity 3.1.

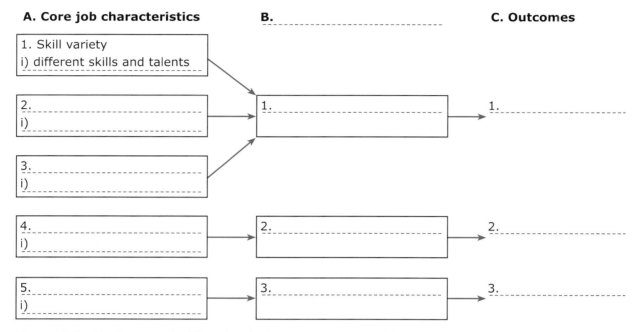

Figure 3.2 Hackman and Oldham's job characteristics model (Source: Arnold, J., Cooper, C. L. and Robertson, I. T. (1995) *Work Psychology: Understanding Human Behaviour in the Workplace* (2nd edn), London, Pitman, p. 395, Figure 19.1)

Comment

If you compared your answers with those of other students, you might have found some minor differences. But the main concepts of Hackman and Oldham's job characteristics model should be reasonably clear from this activity.

In the next activity, you will rewrite your personal experience text using Hackman and Oldham's concepts to frame it.

Activity 3.4

Purpose: to write a personal experience text framed by business studies concepts.

Task 1: read the text you produced in Activity 3.2, using the completed diagram from Figure 3.2 to frame your reading.

(a) How many of the concepts in the diagram have you given examples for in your text?

(b) How many of the concept words in the diagram have you used in your text?

(c) How does the organisation of your text compare with the organisation of the diagram?

Task 2: now rewrite your job description, using the concepts from Figure 3.2 to frame it. There is no advice about how you should do this. You must decide on the organisation and language style you use.

There is no answer for this activity because it is personal to you.

3.4 Skills-evaluation reports

In this section you will read the first of several self-evaluation reports by students. Throughout their course, students were asked to audit their skills each time they wrote an assignment. They were expected to focus on one or two skills and pay special attention to developing them during the course. The reports you will read were written at the end of the course.

Here is the learning outcome from the business studies course which the first report addresses:

By the end of this module you should be able to demonstrate that you can:

Combine information from the course Reader, research, and your own experience to illustrate what **business processes** *are.*

(From *Understanding Business Behaviour: Processes*)

Although it is not exactly the same, this outcome relates to the following two outcomes of LB160 *Professional communication skills for business studies.*

Key skills:

3   *select data, information and ideas from different sources and present them in an appropriate fashion to support an argument.*

Practical and/or professional skills:

2   *identify and communicate potential solutions based on knowledge of theory, and apply it to your own work situation.*

Skills-evaluation reports like these often have a problem–solution pattern. The **problem** is the absence of a skill or a weakness in it. The **solution** is a development of the skill. The **evaluation** is an account of how effective the development has been. Problem, solution and evaluation are all **claims**. Like a claim in an argument, they need some kind of basis. Often the basis used is **evidence**, that is, an example from the writing that the student has done on the course. **Evaluation** occurs throughout the text.

Activity 3.5 ....

Purpose: to introduce a self-evaluation report – its content, organisation and language.

Task 1 Content: Text 3.3 in Resource Book 3 is a self-evaluation report by a student (Anna) reflecting on her use of personal experience in her business studies writing. Read Text 3.3 and then answer the following questions.

(a) What kind of evidence does Anna present to support her claim that she had problems using personal experience in her business studies writing?

(b) Do you believe her?

(c) This self-evaluation report is part of a portfolio of work that Anna hands in at the end of the course. Can you suggest what evidence she could include to convince you that she had problems using personal experience in her writing?

(d) What evidence does Anna present to support her claim that she has improved in using her personal experience in business writing?

(e) What other evidence could she have presented?

(f) Even though Anna seems to have solved her original problem with using personal experience in her writing, she points out that there are still problems. What are these problems? Why do you think she points them out?

Task 2 Organisation: read through the text to see how Anna organised her report. In the right-hand column, write the words Problem, Solution, Evidence or Evaluation wherever you can see her writing about them. You should find that she moves around these four stages in various sequences. (She does not necessarily write about them in the order given here.) It may not always be clear whether a stage is a problem, evidence or evaluation. Don't worry about this; just make the decision that seems most reasonable to you. The first paragraph is done for you as an example.

Task 3 Language: underline the main *self-evaluation words* and *word groups* which Anna uses in her report. The words in the first paragraph are underlined as an example.

Compare your answers with those suggested in the Answer section.

Comment ....

Anna organises her reflection to persuade her tutor that she has made progress in the skills she reflects on. By identifying a weakness, and then describing actions she has taken to solve this problem, she presents an argument about her own development. The facts in her reflection are undoubtedly true but the important skill she uses to write this reflection is presenting the facts persuasively. She loses some strength in her argument by not referring to actual texts which show the problem she is describing. However, her argument is successful when she refers to the assignment in which she solves the problem, and to her tutor's positive feedback on the assignment. She also demonstrates a critical attitude to her own development, which is a persuasive move. For this reflection Anna was awarded a high mark.

Extract 3.4 in Resource Book 3 is an extract from the assignment Anna refers to, in which she uses her personal experience. How does her description of her personal experience compare with the one you wrote for Activity 3.4?

3.5 Organisation of skills-evaluation reports

Anna's text is a report on how her skills developed during a business studies course. To write an effective skills-development report like this, Anna organises the report using a problem–solution pattern like the one shown in Figure 3.3.

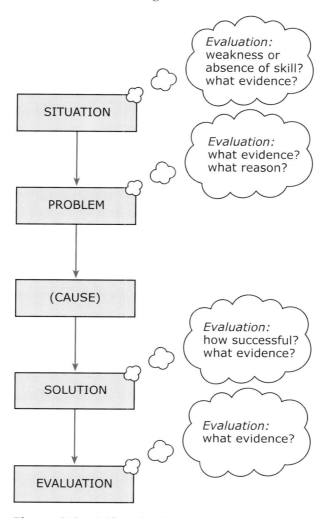

Figure 3.3 Self-evaluation pattern

As Figure 3.3 shows, each evaluation should be based on evidence. As mentioned already, you may not necessarily present the text in the sequence shown – but most evaluation texts will include some kind of problem, solution, evaluation and evidence.

3.6 Argument in skills-evaluation reports

Self-evaluation reports are personal. They are about your experience. However, like other reports, they are also public documents, written for someone else to read – usually a tutor. For that reason, they need to be organised and expressed in ways that will influence their audience.

As you have seen, self-evaluation reports have an argument structure and, in particular, depend on the convincing use of evidence. In this section you will look at how students present an argument. The reports in this section are self-evaluations of a different set of skills: **skills in using models and diagrams in business studies writing**. These are the skills you practised in Session 2.

The students who wrote these reports focused on their development of the following undergraduate business skills.

The ability to:

- use models to describe business environments.
- apply given models to specific examples of business environments.
- prepare material which represents information diagrammatically.
- use diagrammatic representations to organise large amounts of information and aid understanding of content.

To understand the reports in the following activities, it is important, first, to be clear about the relationship between business models and business diagrams.

Activity 3.6

Purpose: to understand the relationship between business models and business diagrams.

Task: read Extract 3.5 in Resource Book 3. Use this information and think back to the reports you worked with in Session 2. Identify which diagrams in Session 2 were models and which diagrams were not. Make three short lists of the models and diagrams in Session 2: (1) models which were also diagrams; (2) models which were not diagrams; and (3) diagrams which were not models.

Compare your answers with those suggested in the Answer section.

Comment

There is an overlap between the skills of using business models and using business diagrams. But they are not necessarily the same thing. It will be useful to bear this in mind when you look at the reports that follow.

In the next activity you reflect a little more on your use of models and diagrams in Session 2.

Activity 3.7

Purpose: to produce a self-evaluation report on your ability to use models and diagrams in business studies.

Task: think back to your experience of using business models and diagrams in Session 2. In general, how would you evaluate your use of models and diagrams? Were you already familiar with using them? Do you find them easy to use? In general, in your writing, how have you developed your ability to use models and diagrams? How did your skills in using models and diagrams develop in Session 2? Write your reflections on these questions as a short report. Save this first draft. You will need it again when you do Activity 3.9.

There is no answer for this activity because it is personal to you.

Comment

As made clear in Extract 3.5, models are important in business studies. Usually, they provide thinking tools for analysing the business environment more effectively. Working with diagrams is often part of using models, but not everyone finds this easy. In the next activity you will read a student's report on how her ability to use both models and diagrams developed during her study.

Activity 3.8 ....

Purpose: to understand a student's experience of using models and diagrams in business studies.

Task: read Sandy's self-evaluation report in Text 3.6 of Resource Book 3. Then answer the following questions.

1 Sandy was critical of her use of models previously. Why?

2 Give an example of how you think Sandy used models in the past and how she uses them now after this course? If you are not sure about this, return to this question after you have read through her self-evaluation again.

3 What does Sandy think is the connection between IT and models? Do you agree? Do you work in the same way?

4 In what ways do the first three diagrams (Figures 1, 2 and 3) demonstrate Sandy's skills development?

5 What do you think Sandy means by *non-pictorial presentation of models*?

6 Have you got any examples of models *making complex ideas fathomable and theories applicable* from your own experience? If so, write down one or two of these examples. How do they compare with Sandy's model in Assignment 05?

7 What do you think Sandy means when she criticises herself for not having a *structured plan*?

8 How do you think using models has helped her develop *different methods of communicating*?

9 How does Sandy intend to continue developing her skills with models?

10 Do you expect Sandy's manager is likely to encourage her interest in models? Or will the manager see it as just an academic interest and not relevant to the workplace?

Compare your answers with those suggested in the Answer section.

Comment ....

Sandy has organised her experiences in this self-evaluation report so that her tutor – and other readers – can easily see her academic and professional development. The report is part of a Skills Portfolio from the business course she is studying. It was written in response to the set of guidelines below.

Guidelines for writing a skills evaluation

Choose one of the skills you have worked on developing during the course and in a statement of not more than 500 words:

1 explain what you did to improve in your chosen skill area

2 analyse the effectiveness of your approach (could a different strategy have resulted in further improvements?)

3 identify any further work you could undertake to improve in this area (you should mention sources of support which you might use, for example study skills books) and explain how this could make up part of your strategy for future study.

The next activity is an extended activity in which you will look at how Sandy has responded to this task. The purpose of the activity is to familiarise you with the organisation and language of an effective self-evaluation report as preparation for writing one yourself. You will focus on the following features of the report.

Introduction

Describing skills

Evaluating development

Making claims about performance

Supporting claims with evidence

Planning future development

Before you look more closely at Sandy's self-evaluation report, look at Text 3.7 in Resource Book 3. This is the front cover and contents page of Sandy's entire Skills Portfolio. The report you are focusing on in these activities is Part C of the portfolio. The page numbers in Sandy's report are pages where she included evidence of the skills she has developed.

Activity 3.9

Purpose: to become familiar with the organisation and language of a self-evaluation report in preparation for writing your own.

Note: you should not wait until the end of this long activity to look at the Answer section. Refer to it as you work through the various tasks.

Introduction

Task 1: often, the opening sentence identifies the skill to be evaluated. Look at the start of Text 3.6 in Resource Book 3. What words does Sandy use to identify the skill to be evaluated?

Task 2: Extract 3.8 is a selection of opening sentences from other self-evaluation reports. Which one of these is most similar to Sandy's opening sentence? How does the opening sentence you wrote in Activity 3.7 compare with these?

Task 3: a skill has probably been chosen for development because the student has a problem with it. In Sandy's opening paragraph (Text 3.6), what words does she use to show she has a problem with this skill? Why does she have this problem?

Task 4: look at the opening sentences in Extract 3.8 again. Which sentences identify a problem with the skill the writers are focusing on? Which of these problem sentences is most similar to Sandy's? Do any of the writers in Extract 3.8 explain why they have a problem? Did you identify a problem in your report in Activity 3.7?

Compare your answers with those suggested in the Answer section.

Comment

Sandy's self-evaluation report has a problem–solution pattern. In the opening paragraph, she identifies the problem which she will solve in the rest of the report.

Describing skills

Task 5: skills are actions and so it is natural to write about them using *verbs*. For example:

I can use models to describe business environments.

However, it is often useful in self-evaluation reports to use *nouns* or *noun groups* to describe skills. For example:

> The use of models to describe business environments is an important skill.

There are two main reasons why Sandy uses nouns or noun groups to refer to skills in her report.

(a) To show what she has focused on or developed. This can be seen in the following two sentences.

> I have focused on the skill of using models to describe business environments;
>
> I need to develop a more accurate method of creating models.

In these sentences the skill is at the end of the sentence; it is part of the point of the sentence.

(b) To make the skill the theme of the sentence and then to make a point about the skill. The following two sentences show examples of this technique.

> Use of models in a previous study had only been to describe situations.
>
> The development of my skill with models has complemented the development of other skills.

In these sentences the skill is at the beginning of the sentence.

Find some more places in Sandy's report where she refers to skills as nouns. Decide whether they are examples of (a) or (b) above.

Task 6: look at the sentences from a range of self-evaluation reports in Extract 3.9. Underline the **nouns** used to refer to the skills evaluated. Decide whether they are examples of (a) or (b) above. (**Note:** these reports are not all about the use of business models.)

Task 7: look again at the report you wrote for Activity 3.7. Underline any skills that you referred to as nouns in the report. Underline in a different colour any skills you have kept as **verbs**. What effect do you think it has on the style of the report if you refer to skills as nouns more than as verbs?

Compare your answers with those suggested in the Answer section.

Comment ....

When referring to skills using verbs, it is usually necessary to use the personal pronoun, *I*. This is perfectly acceptable in self-evaluation reports and, as you have seen, in other kinds of business studies writing too. But using the kinds of nouns you have just identified can give a more formal voice to these personal reports. Sometimes this may help to support the argument.

Evaluating your development

Task 8: in a skills-evaluation report, it is important to demonstrate that you have developed the skills you are describing. You can do this by, first, evaluating weaknesses in your skills and the impact this has on your performance, for example:

> (a) my skill level was <u>initially low.</u>

Then you can describe the actions you took to develop the skills.

> (b) I then took <u>Coates' economy model</u> and <u>developed this</u> to present and simulate part of the economy of a developing country, again <u>stretching my understanding of IT to present a concept clearly</u>.

Finally, you can evaluate the impact of the development on your performance.

> (c) By practising using models and stretching my intellectual under-standing and application of them, <u>I have developed a high level of skill in this area</u>, which I believe to be a <u>fundamental aspect of business studies</u> because models make complex ideas fathom-able and theories applicable.

In a different colour, underline any other examples of (a), (b) or (c) you can find in Sandy's report (Text 3.6).

Compare your answers with those suggested in the Answer section.

Task 9: look again at your report from Activity 3.7. Have you written any examples of the three types of evaluation referred to in Task 8? Can you see any way of increasing the amount of evaluation you have included? If so, write some new sentences to do this.

Comment ....

To evaluate your skill development in a convincing way, it is helpful to recognise what sort of values your reader will think are relevant. Sandy includes evaluation words, which shows that she has a good understanding of what kind of development is relevant in business studies.

Making claims about your performance

Task 10: your evaluations are claims about your performance. The following examples show how Sandy makes claims in her report:

> (a) it <u>became clear</u> that the use of models was imperative
>
> (b) which <u>I believe</u> to be a fundamental aspect of business studies
>
> (c) I think this would have focused my attention on improving even more this aspect of my work and may have resulted in a better mark.

Texts 3.10–3.14 in Resource Book 3 are examples of other students' self-evaluation reports. Read through some of them and identify ways in which the writers make claims about their performance. Write down a list of expressions which can be used for making claims about performance.

Supporting claims with evidence or explanation

Task 11: to make convincing claims, you must have a basis for them. There are three main ways of giving the basis for your claims. The following examples are from Sandy's report.

(a) Show – or describe – an example:

> Further examples of using models are <u>on pages 39 and 41</u>. Non-pictorial presentation of models was also developed in <u>Assignment 03</u>. My preparation for this is <u>on pages 17–21.</u>

(b) Refer to tutor (or colleague) feedback:

> Although my tutor refined the model slightly, it received 'excellent' feedback.

(c) Explain why you make the claim:

> I have developed a high level of skill in this area, which I believe to be a fundamental aspect of business studies <u>because models make complex ideas fathomable and theories applicable</u>.

Again read through some of the sample reports in Texts 3.10–3.14 and find examples of these three ways of supporting a claim.

Did you give the basis for the claims you made in your report in Activity 3.7? How did you do this?

There are no answers for Tasks 9–11 because they are personal to you.

Comment ....

A self-evaluation report, like an essay, is an argument. Writers attempt to convince their readers that the development they describe has happened. The claims in self-evaluation reports are made in more direct and personal language than they are in academic essays and reports. As a result, they depend even more on supporting evidence.

Planning future development

Task 12: it is common for a skills-evaluation report to end with proposals for future development. If the report has followed a problem–solution pattern, this is where writers must be self-critical again. Although they have 'solved' a problem by transforming a weakness into a strength, they are expected to end with a new problem – or opportunity – for development. Sandy introduces that part of her report in the final paragraph:

> To further improve my use of models, <u>I need to develop ...</u>

Look through the rest of Sandy's final paragraph and underline the other expressions she uses to refer to her plans for the future.

Compare your answers with those suggested in the Answer section.

Comment ....

Activity 3.9 was designed to focus on how one student wrote an influential self-evaluation report. She organised her report by carefully following the guidelines given to her in the assignment. In effect, these were the terms of reference for her report. The broad structure of the report is a problem–solution one. She identified a need and demonstrated how she solved it. In writing this report, she used the language skills you identified in this activity.

The purpose of looking at this student's report is not to suggest that this is the only way to write about using models in business studies. Different writers write in different ways. The purpose of looking at other writers' texts is to learn from the comparison with your own. In the next activity you compare some other reports with Sandy's to note how they are similar and how they are different. After that activity, you will consider the question of how writers establish an individual identity in their writing.

Activity 3.10 ....

Purpose: to compare some self-evaluation reports.

Task: Texts 3.10–3.14 in Resource Book 3 are self-evaluation reports.

(a) Look quickly through some of them. Do they generally seem to follow a problem–solution pattern?

(b) Set up a page in your notebook or on your computer with the following headings from Activity 3.9.
Introduction
Describing skills
Evaluating development
Making claims about performance
Supporting claims with evidence
Planning future development

Read through some of the reports and, under the headings, make a note of any words or expressions from the reports that you think are interesting or might be useful in writing your self-evaluation.

(c) Revise the report you wrote in Activity 3.7 in the light of the last three activities. The terms of reference for this report are not exactly the same as for the reports you have read. However, it should be possible to produce an improved draft.

There is no answer for this activity because it is personal to you.

Comment ....

One aspect of reports which this activity might have demonstrated is that reports can 'sound' different. Because self-evaluations are personal, it may be easier for the writer's personality to come across than in more formal academic writing. The next section explores this idea of personality or 'voice'.

3.7 Voice in skills-evaluation reports

There are two ways in which writers show something of their personality, identity or voice. One is through what they say about themselves or the world around them. The other is how they say it. This session began by looking at what personal experience students used in their business studies writing. The previous section looked at very personal accounts by students of their experience as learners. In both these cases, what students write about their experience says something about them as people. In this final section on students' self-evaluation reports, you will pay some attention to the voices students use when they write self-evaluations and when they write more formal academic texts.

The main point of this section is to recognise that people write in different voices. This course emphasises that writing should be adapted to the situation and the audience. However, it should also recognise that writers who adapt to a situation still make choices about how much of their identity or personality they bring into their writing. The next activity explores that.

The self-evaluation reports you will now consider focus on a different set of skills – **note making** and **assignment writing**. You will read two students' self-evaluation reports and compare their voices in these reports with their voices in the essays they wrote.

Activity 3.11

Purpose: to note how writers adapt their voices to different texts.

Task 1: in this activity you will read self-evaluation reports and short essays written by two students. Look fairly quickly through Texts 3.15 and 3.16 in Resource Book 3, and find examples of the items in the table below.

	Student A (Text 3.15)	Student B (Text 3.16)
What they write about 1 Recognition of own weaknesses 2 References to success, failure or difficulty 3 Sources of human or written advice or help		
How they write about it 4 Verbs where 'I' is the subject 5 Words or expressions you think are personal to the writer in some way		

Task 2: bearing in mind the features you identified in Task 1, read fairly quickly through the two essays in Texts 3.17 and 3.18. Then decide which student wrote which essay. Use any clues from the organisation and the language style of the texts to help you.

	Reason(s) for decision
Student A wrote Text ...	
Student B wrote Text ...	

Compare your answers with those suggested in the Answer section.

Comment ....

From this activity you should note that readers form impressions and opinions of writers based on their voice, and that writers' gender, background and political opinions often come through their words without their even being conscious of it. By developing awareness of your voice you are more likely to make the kind of impression that you want to.

3.8 Writing a skills-evaluation report

Activity 3.12 ....

Purpose: to write a skills-evaluation report.

Task: using the learning outcomes in Text 3.1 and the notes you made in Activity 3.1, choose a skill that you have developed during this course and write a report on that development. Write about 500 words. Pay attention to the way in which you use the problem–solution text organisation and construct the argument, and try to be conscious of your voice.

There is no answer or comment for this activity because it is work that will be assessed.

3.9 Conclusion

This session has looked at skills audits which are produced on business studies courses. For writers who are used to more impersonal writing styles, such skills audits can seem difficult to produce. However, they are similar to other reports in that they have an organisation and language style which are adapted to their purpose and audience. They also present an opportunity to develop a more personal voice in professional writing.

3.10 Review

In this session you should have:

- developed your understanding of how skills audits are structured for their audience and purpose
- developed the language of evaluation used in skills audits
- developed skills in using your personal experience, both in academic writing and as the basis for self-evaluation
- learned more about the use of formal and informal, and personal and impersonal language in documents
- written a skills-evaluation report.

3.11 Answer section

Activity 3.5

Task 1 Content

(a)   A description of her personal experience: *I had struggled and prevaricated for quite a while ...*

(b)   There is no indication in the text that Anna shouldn't be believed but your answer may differ.

(c)   Anna could have presented some texts she had written where it would have been useful to include personal experience but she had not.

(d)   Anna includes a description of her personal experience and a reference to the positive feedback she got from her tutor.

(e)   She could have presented some example texts.

(f)   There is a possibility that Anna presents opinions based on personal experience that is too narrow. There is also continuing uncertainty about how much personal experience to include. She probably points out the first problem to demonstrate that she is aware of a real danger; it also gives her the chance to refer to the development of critical thinking skills, which is another very positive aspect of her skills development. The recognition of continuing uncertainty about how much personal experience to use is an example of how Anna continues to be reflective about her performance. This is a positive aspect to demonstrate.

Task 2 Organisation and Task 3 Language

	Stage
Self-evaluation of the following business graduate skill: **Combine information from Reader articles, knowledge and research, and your own experience to illustrate understanding of business concepts.**	
I was <u>very pleased</u> with my efforts at the above skill from the module on Business Processes. Whilst I had found it relatively straightforward to include information from Reader articles and research into my writing, <u>I had found it much harder to decide</u> when, where and how much personal experience and knowledge to include. <u>I had struggled and prevaricated</u> for quite a while on how to incorporate my own experience into my writing.	Evaluation Problem Evidence
<u>I feel that I was successful</u> in this skill <u>as I found it very easy to</u> relate the module to my own experiences. So, when I was writing Assignment 04, and had an overview of the module, <u>I found it easy to</u> use my own previous work experience in the assignment. At the same time, <u>it was difficult to</u> know how much personal reflection to include, and <u>I was worried</u> that personalising my writing <u>would detract from</u> an attempt	Evaluation Evidence Problem

at an 'academic' piece of writing. When I am making notes, I try and relate the subject matter to examples from my experience to aid understanding and enable me to remember details, but <u>I was wary of</u> including this in more formal writing. In fact, including my own experience <u>made the essay much easier to</u> write, as <u>I found</u> my writing <u>flowed much better</u>, and by using examples <u>it was easier to</u> explain the points I was trying to make.

    Problem

    Evaluation of solution

    Evidence

Developing my skills in Assignment 4 and the <u>positive feedback</u> received has shown me that personal experience <u>can and should be included</u> in my writing. However, this must also be balanced by the fact that <u>my experience could be limited</u> in certain areas, and <u>it would be easy to</u> make generalisations and assumptions <u>which do not have a wide enough basis</u>. On the other hand, my study has shown me that theories and models can be questioned, and there is no 'right' answer. As I have progressed through the readers and study guide the conflicting views of theorists, combined with my own experience <u>has demonstrated that</u> all viewpoints should be questioned. I feel this is a skill that <u>I need to develop further</u> in my studies, and <u>I need to work on</u> my critical thinking skills.

    Evidence

    Evaluation

    Problem

    Evaluation

    Solution

    Evidence

    Problem

Even after successfully using this skill for Assignment 04 <u>I am still hesitant to</u> put my own experience into my writing. <u>I found</u> the answer for the self-evaluation in Assignment 06 Part B <u>quite difficult to</u> complete, as I had to put a lot of personal reflection into the self-evaluation. However, it has been <u>a valuable process to</u> reflect on my skills, and the areas of my study that have gone well, and not so well. Time for reflection is not something I normally do (poor time management again!), but the study skills sheets have forced me to think about the skills I have and challenges I face. The fact that I am more aware of my skills and areas that need to be improved <u>will put me in a stronger position</u> in November for my next course.

    Problem

    Evidence

    Evaluation

    Solution

Activity 3.6

1　**Models which were also diagrams:** exchange relationship; Porter's Five Forces Model; STEEP analysis; Porter's value chain; SWOT analysis.

2　**Models which were not diagrams:** all the models were also diagrams – but not all the models are presented as diagrams.

3　**Diagrams which were not models:** staffing structure; proportions of investors in China; Kazakhstan market summary; Japanese visitors; budget allocations in African countries; experience of call centres; origin of informal traders (although this last one could be seen as an informal model).

Activity 3.8

1   Sandy used models to describe situations but not to analyse or synthesise them. In other words, she was not really using models to help her think about business situations and explain why events happened the way they did.

2   Perhaps Sandy means she used models – or rather flow diagrams – in a descriptive way to show the processes inside an organisation. This kind of diagram is a representation of a business process but does not organise information about the business in the same way that Mintzberg's cast of players model does. One reason for this is the use of categories to organise information in the Mintzberg diagram. You have to think about which category a stakeholder belongs to and what their relationship is with stakeholders in other categories.

3   Sandy thinks that IT can help her create the diagrams she uses to represent business models. Many people find that computer-created diagrams help with thinking about business studies ideas – although time has to be spent on understanding the software to create these diagrams. Sandy clearly thinks the time is well spent.

4   Assignment Diagram 1 is technically simpler than the next two. Diagram 2 is technically skilful. But, with Diagram 3, Sandy seems to have been both technically skilled but also intellectually skilled. She says she has adapted the original model to represent something different from what it was originally designed to do.

5   Sandy probably means the difference between business models and business diagrams. For example, it is possible to write about the 'hard' and 'soft' models of human resource management. However, it is not necessary to draw a picture or diagram to show how these models work. They can be described in words, or in a simple table.

6   The kinds of concept map which were introduced earlier in this course can make complex ideas fathomable. But often a concept map cannot be used as a business model. The relationships between the concepts are personal to you and might not be the same for another person. Sandy's model in Assignment 05 appears to be based on relationships which are more systematically organised.

7   Sandy believes that she should have SMART development targets which are Specific, Measurable, Agreed, Realistic and Timed. In other words, she thinks she should be systematic in how she develops herself.

8   Sandy probably means that the diagrams are an alternative to words. She may also mean that the models provide categories and concepts which other people know or can learn. For example, Mintzberg's 'face diagram' can help other people understand the relationships between stakeholders even without the visual diagram in front of them.

9   Sandy appears to have a very dynamic understanding of models and intends to explore how she can create original models herself.

10   The manager is very likely to encourage Sandy. Most modern businesses would probably support this kind of professional development and not see it as 'too academic'. Of course, this would depend to some extent on her role in the company.

Activity 3.9

Introduction

Task 1

I have particularly focused on the skill of using models.

Task 2

I decided to focus on or I have chosen to concentrate on

Task 3

This is because my skill level was initially low as I had little experience of using models.

Task 4

Being fairly new to academic study [explanation for problem] there were many areas where improvement was required to become a successful learner.

My greatest weakness is in using models and diagrams

One area that I considered to be weak with my study was the ability to organise my note taking

None of these sentences is exactly like Sandy's opening. The most similar are probably *My greatest weakness is in using models and diagrams* and *this was the skill with which I chose to work.*

Describing skills

Task 5

(a)   The skill of using models to describe business environments; experience of using models; application of models in Assignment 2; my understanding of models; the development of my skill with models.

(b)   Use of models in previous study; the use of models was imperative; further examples of using models; non-pictorial presentation of models; using diagrammatic representation; a more accurate method of creating models; undertaken during the development of models.

Task 6

(a)   I found using mind maps very useful when planning essays.

At this stage of my study I am not aware of any other methods for planning and organising written work so I cannot assess if a different method suits my study work.

Assignment 05 was my first attempt at organising the material into sections marked by headings and subheadings.

(b)   <u>Being able to simplify descriptions of models</u> enabled me to progress onto understanding theories.

<u>Studying the diagrams presented in the readers</u> has assisted me in understanding the material presented.

<u>Making more use of flow charts to show processes</u> should make studying easier and assist in note taking.

<u>The three stages of extracting key points, sorting them into logical groups and developing sentences from the key points</u> enabled me to plan and organise the points extracted from the chapters.

However, <u>ensuring that sufficient referencing details were logged with the notes</u> would have further improved the strategy.

<u>Lack of discipline</u> was the learning skills weakness I chose to focus on.

Task 7

It is likely to make the report sound more formal and impersonal.

Evaluating your development

Task 8

(a)   it was not always done with a structured plan

(b)   I sought to develop this beyond the skills audit.

I had the confidence to attempt my own model to show a relationship between levels of control in bureaucratic organisations.

(c)   I think this would have focused my attention on improving even more this aspect of my work and may have resulted in a better mark.

The development of my skill with models has complemented the development of a wide range of skills.

Planning future development

Task 12

Over the next two to three years <u>I will research</u> ...

At my next personal development review <u>I intend to discuss</u> with my manager in-house training options for this.

Activity 3.11

Task 2

Student A wrote Text 3.17; student B wrote Text 3.18.

SESSION 4 Email communication in the workplace

4.1 Introduction

One of the aims of this course is to enhance your ability to communicate with other people in the workplace. This session examines how emails are used for workplace communication.

The systems model of writing business documents which has been used throughout this course can be adapted to show emails as one type of workplace document.

Figure 4.1 shows how a workplace document is produced. It begins with the *inputs* which drive the writing process. These may include the context in which you work, your purpose for communicating, the action you hope to achieve as a result, the audience that you are trying to reach, and the ideas that you want to disseminate. These inputs influence the *process* involved, such as selecting a suitable mode of communication and style of language. Finally, there are the *outputs* in the form of letters, emails, reports, proposals, and so on.

Workplace communication may be internal or external. Internal communication involves the employees within an organisation, while

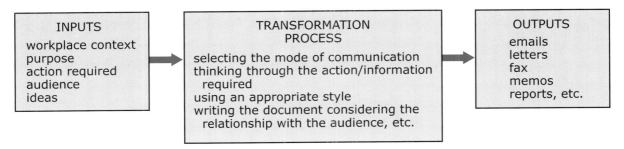

Figure 4.1   A systems model of writing workplace documents

external communication is between the people inside and those outside it. The external audience may include clients, suppliers, supporters and regulators.

Activity 4.1

Purpose: to consider the various possible means of communication in the workplace.

Task: think about the organisation that you work for. Consider the various ways that, as an employee, you communicate with the people within the organisation and those outside it. If you are not in employment, choose an organisation and imagine the ways an employee of that organisation is likely to communicate. Make two lists – one for internal communication, one for external communication. Which of these ways of communication is most commonly used? Why do you think this is?

There is no suggested answer for this activity but you will find feedback in the comment below.

Comment

This reflective activity requires you to draw on your experience of a workplace environment. Among the ways of communication that you might have mentioned are: letters, reports, memos, emails, faxes, oral presentations, telephone, notes and face-to-face conversation.

Some of these may be used primarily for internal communication and others for external communication. This will depend partly on the nature of the organisation and partly on company policy. Among the factors influencing such choices will be cost and effectiveness.

Although various means of communication are used in the workplace, technological advances mean there is a marked tendency to use **online communication**, particularly email, for both internal and external business activity.

Learning outcomes

In this session you will:

- consider the value of different forms of communication in the workplace
- learn about some of the problems inherent in workplace emails
- learn how to overcome those problems
- learn how to organise the content of emails
- develop an understanding of the functions and language of workplace emails.

4.2 Choosing a form of communication

Before discussing emails in more detail, it is worth considering the merits of using other forms of communication in the workplace. These include:

1   personal meetings
2   telephone calls
3   letters
4   faxes.

Meetings are an effective way of both starting and building relationships. When physically in each other's presence, participants subconsciously use visual and auditory cues – such as facial expression, tone of voice and physical distance – to guide their interaction. These cues can provide participants with valuable feedback on others' reaction to what is being said – knowledge that is the first step to learning how to work together.

The fact that these cues are not available in written communication means that face-to-face meetings tend to be more appropriate when dealing with complex issues. Examples of these include persuading someone to do something, discussing poor performance, or raising matters of potential conflict. By being in the physical presence of someone, you are in a better position to assess their feelings as you explore these issues and can adapt your approach as necessary.

Where it is not possible to meet up physically because of geographical distance, the telephone can be a good substitute and tends to be better than email in circumstances such as those outlined above. Telephone calls are also excellent for maintaining a good working relationship, as they allow for a level of connection that is harder to achieve in writing. They can be invaluable when making arrangements such as a business meeting, as they permit both parties to look up dates in their diaries, suggest alternative options and negotiate the exact time and location. To use email to make these kinds of arrangements can be a lengthy process, particularly if several people are involved.

Letters still have a role to play in business. They are a very useful means of initiating business contact. This is partly because they are not so immediately intrusive on the recipient's time as a telephone call or email might be. They can also be used to transmit paper documents, such as proposals or certificates, which are likely to be filed among the recipient's paper records.

Emails have become so commonplace that a letter carries a feeling of sincerity, a sense that the writer has put special effort into composing it. Letters can seem tangible and enduring compared to the ephemeral nature of emails.

At the time of writing (2008), despite a reduction in their use, faxes still retain some functionality in business communication, particularly as regards issues of commitment and confidentiality. If, for example, a hand-signed or confidential document is needed quickly, it can be faxed through in a matter of minutes.

Bearing in mind the advantages and disadvantages of the different forms of communication, the ideal may be to use several in combination with one another.

Nevertheless, it is important to recognise that each company will have its own preferences about channels of business communication. These need to be ascertained, particularly when companies are working together. A mix of different channels of communication can be used at various stages of a project, according to their effectiveness.

4.3 Workplace email communication

This section begins by considering the advantages and disadvantages of email communication (Figure 4.2). It then looks at elements of style and organisation.

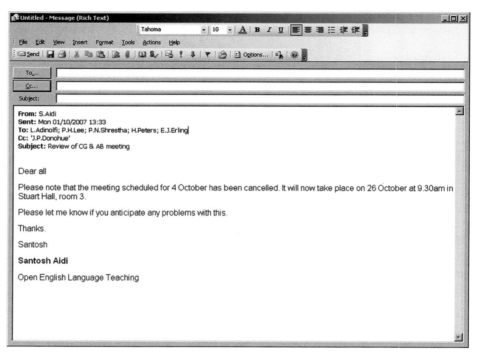

Figure 4.2   An example of a workplace email

Activity 4.2 ....

Purpose: to raise your awareness of the advantages and disadvantages of using emails for workplace communication.

Task: think about the various benefits of using emails in the workplace. Then think about the potential disadvantages of this form of communication. Complete the table below with a list of your ideas. An example is given in each column to get you started.

Benefits	Problems
Quick and easy to use	Potentially intrusive

Compare your answers with those suggested in the Answer section.

You will now explore some of the disadvantages of email communication and consider how best to deal with them.

Emails can be intrusive

The immediacy of emails makes them feel like personal communication. However, personal communication in normal, face-to-face settings is a subtle, two-way process. In face-to-face communication, you can quickly sense whether someone wants to engage in conversation with you. Even if they do, you will be able to read the signs as to whether they are interested in the topic you have raised, whether they are distracted, or don't have much time to talk. These signs will help you adapt the conversation accordingly.

An email, in contrast, is delivered into someone's inbox. This entering of the receiver's space can be more intrusive than face-to-face communication. For this reason, each email should be sent with forethought.

Emails can also be potentially disruptive to the recipient's working patterns. It is important to bear in mind that the pressure to respond to messages and the time required to do so can impact considerably on the other work commitments they have to attend to.

Emails may not be private

When you are talking one-to-one with someone, you normally assume that what you are saying can be heard only by you and the person

you are talking to. If you are in a place with other people around, you can move out of earshot.

Because email correspondence can feel like a private conversation, it is easy to write things that you imagine no one else will read. Yet it is probably best to assume that any of the work emails that you send could potentially be read by people other than those to whom they are addressed.

The recipient may be in the middle of reading an email on screen, unaware that it is available for other colleagues to view unintentionally as they walk past. Printed out messages may be accidentally read if mislaid or carelessly disposed of. Another possibility is that the recipient innocently forwards the email to people who they think might be usefully included in the exchange, but who you had not anticipated would read your message. There is also the risk that you might send an email to the wrong person by mistake.

Emails may not be read immediately

When sending emails, it is important to be aware that that your message may not be read immediately. Some people use a type of *read notification* facility – so that they can be alerted when their message has been read, but this does not signal whether the email was simply opened or read in detail. Moreover, requesting this kind of notification from the recipient can sometimes cause offence.

Workplace email systems have an *out-of-office autoreply* facility, which can be used when the recipient is on leave or otherwise away. The *autoreply* message may indicate when the person will be back and whom to contact during their absence.

Emails are not the same as talking or writing letters

The speed at which emails can be sent and received can at times give the illusion that you are having a real conversation with someone.

Nevertheless, it is important to remember that email does not provide the visual and other cues that contribute so much to successful face-to-face communication.

At the same time, because an email comprises words, sentences and paragraphs, it can appear to have all the benefits of a letter.

However, a business letter tends to be a carefully composed document. Its production usually receives considerable thought: thought about its purpose; the organisation of the content; the reaction of the recipient; the style, tone and choice of wording. It may be reviewed by colleagues, who can point out improvements in its content or style. It is checked both before and after being printed out on formal letter-headed paper. All such processes help avoid hastiness before it is sent.

When writing an email, these considerations often disappear. It is all too simple to dash off a message and press the *Send* button. The result is that your message may be unclear or otherwise unprofessional. Most email systems have the option to save your draft so that you can return to redraft and edit it later.

Tips for writing emails

- Think before you press *Send*.
- Be aware that the reader may be reading the email at a later date, and that the resulting action may take place even later – if at all.
- Design your emails so that they contain appropriate time frames for action and, ideally, to elicit confirmation that the action will take place.
- Be prepared to use other forms of communication to follow up – or to address in parallel – the issue that you are writing about.
- Avoid using email if you have difficult matters to talk about and when the subtlety of how the recipient is reacting is important.
- Design your emails so that you clearly signal important shifts in point of view or feeling by starting a new paragraph and making such shifts explicit.

Style of workplace emails

The style of language used in both internal and external workplace emails varies according to:

- the relationship between the sender and the recipient
- the culture of particular organisations.

Activity 4.3 ....

Purpose: to compare two workplace emails.

Task: read Texts 4.1 and 4.2 in Resource Book 3. Note down the main ways in which they are different and underline some examples of these differences.

There is no suggested answer for this activity but you will find feedback in the comment below.

Comment ....

Although both emails have a similar basic structure, each one has a distinctive style. This reflects the relationship between sender and recipient.

Text 4.1 is more like a personal email, since it is informal in style. This is evident in its opening line (*Hi Pete*), and the fact that the sender signs off with his first name only. The text also includes incomplete sentences (e.g. *Just heard about your promotion*), which are a feature of personal messages.

In contrast, Text 4.2 is more formal and impersonal. This is exemplified by the greeting and sign off (*Dear Peter*; *Best wishes*) and the full name of the sender at the end. Not only is the text longer but its sentences are more complex: *I am pleased to inform you that ...*; *In view of this ...*; *Should this not be necessary...*; *I would like to take this opportunity to offer you my congratulations*; *I look forward to hearing from you ...*

Style and cross-cultural communication

The impact of globalisation and online communication has increased the need to be sensitive to cultural diversity. It is most likely that a range of different cultures will be represented within the workplace, community and other groups that you are involved in too.

Broadly speaking, two main types of culture have been identified. These are referred to as **individualist** and **collectivist cultures** (Hofstede, 2001).

Most European, Australian and North American countries are considered to have an individualist culture, while Asian and African countries are examples of a collectivist culture.

Individualist cultures value personal beliefs, rights and independence. Central to business communication in individualist cultures are directness and transparency. Written words are given high importance in this environment.

In contrast, collectivist cultures are typified by group values and loyalty, interdependence and indirectness. In such cultures, the maintenance of trusting relationships is considered more important than business transactions. Furthermore, verbal agreement and non-verbal behaviours are given more significance than written agreements.

English has largely become the **lingua franca** for business communication across languages and cultures. However, even when communicating in the same language, it is important to be aware of the values, beliefs and preferences of the parties involved. Contact with people in a collectivist culture is likely to require a more tactful and considerate choice of language. You will look at this in more detail in later sections.

The organisation of workplace emails

The organisation of workplace emails has many similarities to that of letters, in terms of their key elements and the way in which they are sequenced as follows.

1 A clear subject line

(Note that this is in the *header* section of the email.)

- This should be short, and specify clearly the topic of the mail.
- If the mail deals with two different topics, make sure both are mentioned in the subject line.
- If the mail has been going back and forth using Re: in the subject line, consider updating the topic if this has evolved since the original email and during the exchanges.

2 A salutation

- This is a basic courtesy. Only rarely should it be missed out.
- If you are not sure what form or name to use to address the person, use the same style that the recipient used in any previous messages to you. If you are the first to initiate contact, it is safest to begin by using the recipient's surname (e.g. Dear Ms Kristiansen, Dear Dr Marconi).

3 An introduction

- This is a key feature of the document. Use it to:
  (a) show how the message relates to other contacts with the recipient or the company – whether these took place by telephone, email or in person
  (b) be clear about what the topic is. If there are two separate topics, make sure you mention both in the introduction
  (c) make clear what your purpose is in sending the message.

4 Main message

- Deal with each issue separately and in order.
- The longer the email, the more clearly you should indicate that you are turning to a new item.

5 Action statements

- Say what you will do and what the recipient should do, as appropriate.
- If there are any time constraints, mention these explicitly.
- It can also be helpful to make it clear that no action is required: for example, *there is nothing you need to do for the time being*).

6 *Closing statement*

- This is optional but it can be helpful in ensuring that the message does not end too abruptly. Examples of closing statements include phrases such as *I look forward to hearing from you soon* or *Thank you in advance for your attention to this matter.*

7 *Farewell statement*

- This is a basic courtesy, like saying *goodbye* when you finish talking to someone.
- Farewell statements can range from the very informal (*Cheers*), through to fairly neutral (*Yours, Best wishes*) to more formal (*Yours sincerely, Kind regards*). If you are not sure which form to use, copy the style that the recipient has used in previous correspondence with you.

8 *Your name*

- You may use your first name or your full name. Again, if you are not sure what is most appropriate, use the same style that the recipient has used when signing off previous emails.
- If you want to move to a more informal relationship (by using first name terms), this is where you initiate it.

9 *Your contact details*

- Details such as your job title, the name of the company you work for and relevant contact details can be helpful to the recipient. Not only do these details make it clear what role you have in the organisation, but also they can facilitate alternative forms of contact – by telephone or letter, for example. Such details can be set up and inserted automatically at the end of a message. It is not necessary to include them more than once in a series of emails, however. They may also be omitted for colleagues with whom you are in regular and close contact.
- If you are not available at your usual contact number, because you are on a trip abroad, for example, mention this in the message, after the action statements.

Activity 4.4

Purpose: to check the basic structure of an email.

Task: read the work email below and check which of the above elements it contains. In the right-hand column label the different parts of the message. An example is provided to start you off.

Compare your answers with those suggested in the Answer section.

Subject: New invoice and proposal	*Subject line*
Dear Kirsty	Salutation
Thank you for your message confirming receipt of our invoices.	
On Monday I sent you another invoice for the work done for Mr Evans, together with a proposal for work for Mr Lee. I wondered if I could ask you two favours in relation to these.	
Firstly, we would be grateful if the invoice for Mr Evans could be paid at the same time as the others you have received. This would be of enormous help to us.	
Secondly, we would appreciate it if Mr Lee could sign the proposal and return it to us as soon as possible, to enable the work to start next week as requested.	
Please could you let me know whether you have been successful with regards to these two issues, ideally by the end of today? I will try to call you at about 4.30 pm if I haven't heard from you by then.	
Thank you in advance for your help.	
Best wishes	
Abigail Walker	
Head of Finance	
Myers Building and Contracting	
Tel. 0131 723	

You will now look at some of the above elements in more detail.

Introduction

The introduction is an important element of an email. This is because it informs or reminds the reader of the topic and the purpose of the communication. This prepares them for what is to follow.

Activity 4.5   ....

Purpose: to be able to identify inadequate introductions in emails.

Task: look at the email introductions below. They all fail to give a complete introduction. Edit the mails to improve them. You can invent some information if you need to.

Email A

Here's my report.

Email B

Thanks for your email of early last week in which you asked me to contact you about the schedule for the new ABC training programme. I would now like to send you a provisional timetable.

Email C

You asked me to explain the fees billed to you recently and to draw up a proposal for our accounting work for next year.

Email D

I apologise for my late reply to your email of last week (due to illness). The additional inputs have now been entered. Under Section 4C(b), we have entered 'No', but we are not sure whether this meant you wished for your details to be released to other interested parties or not. Please could you clarify what you meant by your answer?

Email E

The new regulations for early retirement pensions came into effect on January 1, 2006. These regulations restrict certain tax breaks for early retirement schemes.

Email F

We would like to inform you of the following: ...

There is no suggested answer for this activity but there is feedback in the comment below.

Comment

Email A fails for many reasons. The recipient's reactions might include: *What report is this? Did I request it? What am I supposed to do with it? Is it attached to this email?* This demonstrates that you have to be specific when sending a message with an attached document.

Email B may seem acceptable at first sight but it is actually probably responding to an email received the previous week. It would have been courteous to include an apology for the delay in replying.

Email C: although this email refers back to previous communication, it is rather vague in doing so. It could have specified which fees are being referred to, and when, how, and in what context the previous communication took place. The email also combines two different topics in the same sentence: the issue of fees and a reference to a proposal. This is best avoided.

Returning to the issue of fees, because there is a sense that there is a potential problem with this, it might have been more appropriate to make a telephone call to discuss the matter together. Alternatively, a more formal letter might have been suitable, where the details of each party's position could be laid out clearly, with copies of relevant documentation as necessary.

Email D: the initial apology is helpful. However, the main problem is that the paragraph starts to move into details too quickly, without stating clearly what the issues are. What was the topic of the email sent last week? What issues did it raise? What exactly were the inputs? These details need to be made explicit, before each item is fully explained in turn.

Email E: it sounds as if this information may be important for the recipient. However, the email does not explain how the information relates to them, why it is being sent, and whether or not the recipient should act in some way.

Email F: although commonly used, this kind of introductory phrase provides little, or no, useful information. It is better to omit phrases like this and go straight to the point about the matter you want to address.

Action statements

Action statements are another important element of workplace emails. The purpose of an action statement is to clarify what the parties involved can expect from each other. It is not enough to assume that, if an issue is raised, the actions required will be clear. Given that action is a central concern in work environments, it is useful to summarise this again at the end of the message.

Actions can be expressed in various ways.

A typical way of expressing your action as the sender is:

I will ... or I will be + -ing ...

Examples

1   I will arrange for a copy of the plans to be sent to you by courier by the end of today.

2   I will be collecting the publicity leaflets from your warehouse first thing tomorrow morning.

Typical ways of referring to the recipient's action include a range of request expressions, such as:

> Please could you ...?
>
> I understand that you will ...
>
> I hope you will be able to ...
>
> I look forward to + ...ing ...

Examples

1   Please ensure that any requests for equipment you wish to purchase from this budget year are with me by midday, Friday 13th July.

2   I look forward to hearing from you shortly.

The following examples refer to possible action by both the sender and the recipient.

1   Please advise whether you would like me to go ahead and book accommodation for Thursday 12th July.

2   If you don't have a key for your desk, please let me know and I can order one for you.

Functions and language in emails

Workplace emails are primarily concerned with getting things done. As a result, they often contain requests, offers and invitations. These are examples of *functions*.

Because the expressions associated with these functions are used so commonly, they are assumed to be easily understood. However, this is not always the case.

When talking to someone face-to-face or on the telephone, it is usually fairly easy to pick up any misinterpretation thanks to visual or auditory cues. This makes it fairly easy to clarify exactly what was intended.

When you send an email, you do not have any such obvious feedback from the recipient, and so you cannot tell how they have interpreted the message.

Activity 4.6

Purpose: to raise awareness of the multiple meanings that a simple message can carry.

Task: imagine you are sitting at your desk at work. Your line manager approaches you and says, 'Can you come into my office for a few minutes?'

There is no doubt that this is a request. However, there are several different ways of interpreting it. Imagine the different tones of voice she might use or the different expressions on her face. Note down all the ways you might interpret the request.

There is no suggested answer for this activity but there is feedback in the comment below.

Comment ....

The possible interpretations of the above message range from an invitation to pop into her office when it pleases you to an order to join her there immediately, and from an invitation to participate in some casual chat to a possible discussion of your dismissal.

As messages can have multiple interpretations, it is necessary to be aware of such possibilities. You need to try to make your message as explicit as possible.

Activity 4.7 ....

Purpose: to extend your awareness of the possible multiple meanings of emails.

Task: imagine that you have received the following one-line emails. In each case, how would you interpret the message, depending on the context and what you might know about the different senders?

(a) How's the work coming along?

(b) Have you seen the report?

(c) Claire tells me that you're having the day off tomorrow.

(d) Could you ring Mr Evans?

(e) What are you doing at the moment?

There are no suggested answers for this activity but there is feedback in the comment below.

Comment ....

It is important to recognise that the way an email is interpreted by the recipient is not necessarily under your control. To avoid any confusion, however, it is good practice to re-read it carefully, while putting yourself in the recipient's position and considering how they might react to it. This is particularly important when considering cross-cultural differences, as described earlier.

There is a useful technique for reducing the possibility that a message is misinterpreted. This involves inserting some additional text – either before or after the message – to make the meaning clear.

Returning to the example message above: *Can you come into my office for a few minutes?*, the interpretation of this message can be controlled by inserting additional text in the following ways.

> Thank you very much for taking charge of the office while I was away. Can you come into my office for a few minutes? I've got a break now and I'd like to hear how you got on.

> I'm afraid I've had a complaint from the Accounts Department about the data you sent through to them last week. Perhaps you can put me straight on what happened and then I can sort things out with them. Can you come into my office for a few minutes?

The meaning of each version is now considerably clearer and there is much less room for misinterpretation.

4.4 Other forms of online communication

In addition to emails, many organisations use other forms of **online communication** to conduct their business both internally and externally. Examples of these are forums and wikis. Like email, these allow members to communicate in writing at their convenience.

Since these forms of online communication are flexible in terms of time and location, they can be easier to arrange than face-to-face or telephone communication and can therefore enable more people to contribute to the discussion.

Contributing to these written exchanges may be easier for people who might otherwise find group discussions difficult. They also allow more time for reflection, resulting in more considered responses than those of an intense face-to-face meeting.

These forms of communication may not be suitable for making immediate decisions or for discussing serious problems, however.

Online communication does not always need to be written. Software programs such as *Skype* provide the opportunity for real-time audio-visual communication at a distance. Programs such as these enable groups of ten or more to talk with and see each other at a distance. In addition to the main meeting room, they often include a facility for pair or small group discussions in *break-out rooms*. These virtual meetings may also be supplemented by on-screen documents – such as agendas or diagrams. Participants may also use a whiteboard to make notes, along with other facilities for group writing.

4.5 Conclusion

This session has explored the advantages and disadvantages of different forms of communication in the workplace. Its main focus was on the use of workplace emails. It explored aspects of email communication in terms of style, organisation and language. It also gave you opportunities to practise writing workplace emails through several guided activities.

4.6 Review

In this session you have:

- considered the value of different forms of communication in the workplace
- gained an awareness of some of the problems inherent in workplace emails
- learned how to overcome some of the problems
- learned how to organise the content of workplace emails
- developed an understanding of the functions and language that may be used in workplace emails.

4.7 Critical reflection

In your Learning Journal reflect on how communication in your workplace – or another organisation you are familiar with – is influenced by online communication. Consider both the positive and the negative aspects of its use in that particular environment.

4.8 Answer section

Activity 4.2

Benefits	Problems
Quick and easy to use	Potentially intrusive
Independent of time zones	Not always private
Can be cost-effective	May not be read immediately
Flexible: can write to an individual or several people at the same time	No guarantee of response
Useful way of keeping a record of ongoing communication	Potential of offending the recipient unless carefully written
	Managing large numbers of emails can be very time consuming
	Overuse of internal emails can result in a reduction in beneficial face-to-face communication in the workplace

Activity 4.4

Subject: New invoice and proposal	*Subject line*
Dear Kirsty	**Salutation**
Thank you for your message confirming receipt of our invoices.	**Introduction**
On Monday I sent you another invoice for the work done for Mr Evans, together with a proposal for work for Mr Lee. I wondered if I could ask you two favours in relation to these.	Relating to previous contact Topic Purpose of the message
Firstly, we would be grateful if the invoice for Mr Evans could be paid at the same time as the others. This would be of enormous help to us. Secondly, we would appreciate it if Mr Lee could sign the proposal and return it to us as soon as possible, to enable the work to start next week as requested. Please could you let me know whether you have been successful with regards these two issues, ideally by the end of today? I will try to call you at about 4.30 pm if I haven't heard from you by then.	**Main message** and **action statements**
Thank you in advance for your help.	Closing statement
Best wishes	Farewell statement
Abigail Walker	Your name
Head of Finance	Job title/contact details
Myers Building and Contracting	
Tel. 0131 723	

SESSION 5 Marketing and finance documents

5.1 Introduction

In this session, you will work with two different but related types of document: marketing and finance documents. The marketing documents are designed to sell a company, its products or its services. They engage powerfully with customers in persuasive, promotional language. The finance documents are designed to provide an account of a company's finances. They often appear more objective and technical than marketing documents. However, finance documents also seek to engage powerfully with readers and to present the company as positively as possible.

In this session, the activities often ask you to search in other documents for examples of vocabulary and grammar which you should record and use when writing your own documents.

Learning outcomes

In this session you will:

- develop your skills and language in writing short marketing documents
- develop your vocabulary for writing about personal and corporate banking

- develop your skills and language for writing about finance
- write two marketing documents and one finance document.

5.2 Marketing documents

Writing short documents at work

Documents are written tools that help the process of communication within and between organisations and individuals. They are created to do things. They have particular purposes.

Written communication at work may be required to coordinate joint activities within an organisation. It might be involved in setting up relationships with clients and suppliers to make sure that mutual work involved flows smoothly. It might promote the company and its products in the market-place. It may report on business activity for business regulators, investors, or other stakeholders.

In contrast with the texts you have written previously, the texts in this session are read by many people. The writers of marketing and finance texts do not know their readers in the same way as a student knows their tutor. However, this does not mean they have no ideas about who their audience are. On the contrary, writers of marketing texts have knowledge of the market or market segment they are writing for. Writers of financial texts have knowledge of the customers and investors who will read their texts and the legal and **financial regulators** who will monitor what they write.

The features shared by all good documents at work is that they do the job efficiently, communicating clearly and purposefully. The first activity in this session reviews these features.

Activity 5.1 ....

Purpose: to review the features that make documents influential in the workplace.

Task: the list below of features of good workplace documents was created by a Netherlands-based corporate communications organisation. Look through the list and then do the task that follows it.

Good workplace documents should be:

- correct and sufficient in the information they provide
- clearly focused on a specific purpose
- clearly focused on the user of the document
- well organised and well thought through
- readable and concise
- presentable in layout and accurate in writing.

Each feature in this list can be matched with a section of the Influential Document Checklist in the Appendix. Look at the checklist and, next to each feature above, write down a letter (A, B, C, etc.) from the checklist to show which section the feature matches. You may find some features match more than one section of the checklist. If so, write down more than one letter.

Compare your answers with those suggested in the Answer section.

Comment

This list of features means that the majority of documents produced in occupational settings are short. People don't want to spend a lot of time reading when they have other things to do. This principle applies particularly to the documents you will work with next.

Describing to sell

In previous sessions, you looked at how students describe their workplaces as part of longer reports. With marketing texts, and specifically, sales texts, you can see how companies describe themselves.

The texts in this session are written for readers outside the company – they are texts designed to influence customers. In order to *communicate* with customers, it is important to know *who* you are talking to. For this reason, companies spend a lot of time and money on identifying and understanding their customers.

First, you look at some company websites – specifically those of large banks. The primary purpose of such websites is to market the bank and its services.

Activity 5.2

Purpose: to consider one type of customer a business has.

Task: you are probably a customer of a bank. Write a list of what you use the bank for.

There is no suggested answer for this activity but it is discussed in the comment below.

Comment

You probably use a bank to access a current account, which you use to receive money and make payments. You may also have a savings account. Perhaps you have taken out a personal loan or, if you have a house, you may have used the bank to get a mortgage.

When you use a bank for these purposes, you are doing so as a private individual. For the bank, you and people like you form one important group of all their customers. Banks often refer to the services they provide to this group of customers as 'retail banking' or, in their marketing communications, **personal banking**. But a bank has other customers and other services to offer.

Activity 5.3

Purpose: to think about the range of customers and products of a business.

Task: prepare a table with the headings below and list the types of customer that a bank has. Note down a few banking services or products which they might use. An example is done for you. For a few ideas, try browsing the following websites.

Bank of Scotland:	www.bankofscotland.co.uk
Barclays:	www.barclays.co.uk
Co-operative Bank:	www.co-operative bank.co.uk
HSBC:	www.hsbc.co.uk
Lloyds TSB:	www.lloydstsb.com
NatWest:	www.natwest.com
Royal Bank of Scotland:	www.rbs.co.uk

Type of customer	*Type of product or service*
Personal	Accounts, payments (ATMs, cards), loans, mortgages

There are no suggested answers for this activity but it is discussed in the comment below.

Comment

Banks divide their customers into different groups. The groups each bank defines are broadly similar, although the name they give to the group may be different. The major divisions are **Personal Banking**, **Business Banking** and **Corporate Banking**. Personal banking may include a special category for very wealthy customers, referred to as **Private Banking**. Business banking is aimed at companies; it is frequently divided up in terms of how much money the company earns, with the larger customers (£1m or more annual turnover) being catered to by what the banks term Corporate (or, sometimes, Commercial) banking.

How do banks address these different audiences?

The banks address these different audiences in different ways. The reason is that different groups of customer have different **needs** and different **wants**. Needs are what people believe are lacking from their lives; wants are what they perceive can satisfy those needs. For example, you need somewhere to keep your money safe, and so you want a personal bank account. Banks know this and try to get you to open an account at their particular bank.

Personal banking

Activity 5.4

Purpose: to think about how products are offered to a particular market segment.

Task: browse one or two of the bank websites from Activity 5.3. Look at the personal banking pages. Which aspects of their products do the banks emphasise? List some of them.

Comment

Because personal banking is a mass market, there is a strong product orientation. The competitive nature of this market means that banks have to compete with each other for the same customers – and hence any price advantages are given high priority. The websites concentrate on the benefits offered by the product and emphasise the advantages the product has over the products of other banks – without usually mentioning the other banks. Retail customers are, for example, offered 'high' interest on savings accounts, special reductions and periods when they don't have to repay money.

Language for communicating with retail customers – special sentence patterns

The style of the language used to address retail customers is direct. This directness is partly achieved through a variety of special sentence patterns as follows.

- Imperatives: the *Do it!* type of statement is used to tell you what benefit you receive, or what you must do to get it.
- Can: benefits statements beginning with *You can ...*
- Benefits verbs, such as ... *save* ...
- Noun groups: indicate a benefit

- Offers: statements beginning with ... *offers you* ...
- Promises: statements beginning with *We'll* ...
- A word group or **clause** introducing any of the above: *To* ..., *Whatever* ..., *If you* ..., etc.

The next activity gives examples of each of these sentence patterns.

Activity 5.5 ....

Purpose: to develop your awareness of the language features of sales communication.

Task 1: below is a mixed-up list of the sentence patterns that were introduced above. In the table below the list, there is an example for each sentence pattern. Write the name of the pattern next to each example in the table.

imperatives		promises
	noun groups	introductory word groups and clauses
offers	benefit verbs	can

Sentence pattern	Example
	The monthly mortgage repayment calculator **will help** you work out your repayments
	With our ..., **you can get** a great package of benefits.
	The bank's card **offers you** a fantastic rate of interest.
	We'll send you a monthly statement.
	No repayments for three months
	Get 5.5% with our instant access savings account.
	Whether you're new to investments, or an existing customer, you will find ...

Task 2: Text 5.1 in Resource Book 3 is a marketing leaflet for a credit card travel service. Read through it and find further examples of each sentence pattern. Create a table like the one above and add your examples to it.

Task 3: look at one or two web pages for the banks listed in Activity 5.3 describing products for personal customers. Find a few more examples of the sentence patterns listed above and add them to your table.

Compare your answers with those suggested in the Answer section.

Comment ....

This activity uses the technique you have practised during this course for increasing the range of language you use in writing a text. Identifying and recording the language that performs particular functions in a text in this way means that the language is organised and, as a result, more likely to be remembered.

Language for communicating with retail customers – evaluation language

An important feature of promotional marketing texts is very positive evaluative language. This kind of evaluation is one of the major differences between promotional and academic texts. Evaluation is a feature of persuasive academic writing. However, persuasion in academic writing means recognising different viewpoints. In marketing texts, evaluation tends to reinforce one viewpoint: how unique and special the company or product is.

This is achieved by the use of positive vocabulary:

- verbs – verbs describing benefits, e.g. *help you, allow you*
- **adjectives** – special adjectives describing specialness, speed, simplicity, security, etc.
- **adverbs** – special adverbs describing specialness, speed, simplicity, security, etc.
- other words and word groups.

Activity 5.6 ....

Purpose: to help you build your knowledge of evaluative vocabulary used in direct communication with customers.

Task 1: look at Texts 5.2 and 5.3 in Resource Book 3. Find a few examples of the vocabulary types listed above. Create tables with the headings below and add your examples to them. Try to group the vocabulary you collect by topic (an example is given in each table). Before you go on to the next task, compare your answers with the ones suggested in the Answer section.

Task 2: browse one or two pages from a bank's website which describe products for personal customers. Find a few more examples of the vocabulary types listed above and enter them in your tables below. Continue to group the vocabulary you collect by topic.

Verb type	Examples
Benefits	help you, allow you to

Adjective type	Examples
Specialness	special, fantastic

Adverb type	Examples
Ease of use	just

Other phrases – type	Examples
Cheapness	it doesn't have to cost you a penny
Reassurance	peace of mind

Compare your answers with those suggested in the Answer section.

Comment   ....

This activity has shown you that the personal banking market is a mass market. All the banks offer roughly the same products to the same people. Apart from relatively small advantages in price or special offers, the banks can only try to address the consumer directly, emphasising elements of simplicity, security, and so on.

Organising messages into a text

The overall purpose of a marketing text is to predict the customer's needs and wants and persuade the customer that the product will satisfy them. The text does this through **dialogue with the customer.**

In this course, texts have been presented in terms of their audiences and purposes. Even the impersonal and objective language of an academic essay is designed for dialogue with an audience. The difference between an academic essay and a marketing text is that the dialogue with the customer is far more direct and obvious than the dialogue with a course tutor. In order to create a one-to-one dialogue, the voice of a marketing text is often quite personal.

Activity 5.7

Purpose: to examine the organisation and voice of a marketing text.

Task 1: Texts 5.2 and 5.3 are typical examples of retail bank marketing texts. Using the features of marketing texts you have looked at already to help you, write key concept summaries of Texts 5.2 and 5.3 to show how they are organised. For example, the first paragraph of Text 5.2 is organised as follows: **Customer's needs – Benefits of the product**.

Don't be surprised if the text patterns seem repetitive. This is a feature of marketing texts.

Task 2: the repetitive pattern of the texts is one reason why they seem like conversations. Which other language features create the impression that these are personal conversations?

Compare your answers with those suggested in the Answer section.

Comment

The repetitive pattern of question and answer and the language of personal conversation create the impression that this is a dialogue with an individual customer. However, unlike conversations, it is also concise and focused, as workplace documents are expected to be. The organisation and voice of these texts is as carefully planned as an academic essay – but for different purposes and audiences.

The activity above focused on features from Sections B, D and E of the Influential Document Checklist (see Appendix). In the next activity you create a marketing text, using your knowledge of those sections.

Activity 5.8

Purpose: to write a marketing text.

Task 1: imagine that you are setting up a small company providing services or products to the general public. Decide on one or more products or services that you would be interested in providing. If you are working for, or have had experience of working for, a company, you could choose a small range of their products or services (don't try to cover everything). If you don't have any work experience, consider another organisation you know about (an educational organisation, a club or a society), and work creatively. Ask what could the organisation offer to the public? (If you can't think of a type of company or a product, there is a list of ideas that might help you in Text 5.4 in Resource Book 3.)

Task 2: write a short text (up to 500 words long) to promote the company and its products or services. The text can be for publication on a website or in printed form. Pay attention to the features you examined in Activities 5.4–5.6 and Online Activities 5.1 and 5.2. (These are from Sections B, D and E of the Influential Documents Checklist.) Think about, and research if necessary, the products or services offered, who the customers are in each case, what their needs and wants are and how they will benefit from what you offer. Then select what you will write about, decide on how it will be organised and draw up the document.

There are no suggested answers for this activity but see Online Activity 5.3.

Corporate banking

In the next set of activities you will compare the way in which marketing texts designed for the corporate market differ from those aimed at a mass market.

Corporate banking is banking for a different market. It is for very large businesses – those with turnovers in excess of at least £1 million. It should not be confused with Business Banking which is for businesses with turnovers of less than £1 million. Although some of the products offered to large companies are relatively straightforward – after all, a bank account for one company is not that different from a bank account for another company – the banks are looking to increase their earnings by capturing more specialist business from corporate customers. This means that the nature of the approach to a corporate customer differs from the approach to a personal customer.

In the following activities, you will be asked to look at web pages about corporate banking. This is a very specialist topic, and you will probably see many products and services listed that you don't really understand. If you want, you can look up some of the words in a dictionary or find a glossary on the internet. But don't feel you *have* to do this. The activities focus on background language rather than specialist terminology, so you could skim over the more complex terminology.

Activity 5.9

Purpose: to introduce some of the products offered to a different segment of the bank market.

Task: browse through one or two bank websites. This time, look at the corporate banking pages. You may find that different banks use different names for these pages so look for the pages which refer to companies with a turnover in excess of £1 million. Which aspects of their services do the banks emphasise?

Compare your answers with those suggested in the Answer section.

Comment

A few common themes emerge because the banks are trying to sell products and services that are more specialist than the usual bank accounts. Corporate customers will be more persuaded by evidence of expertise and experience than by special offers and cut prices. However, needs, wants and benefits are still important in these more specialised corporate banking texts. Their voice is usually more formal and technical than personal banking texts. The next few activities explore this language further.

Language for communicating with corporate customers

The style of language used to address corporate customers is usually more formal than that used to address personal customers. This formality is shown by the use of:

- more complex word groups, and more complex vocabulary in general
- less use of direct *you*-focused statements
- longer sentences, taking a more descriptive approach and containing more information
- longer paragraphs.

In fact, this style is closer to the language of academic writing than the less formal style of personal banking texts.

Noun groups for products and services

The more formal style for addressing corporate customers requires more specific noun groups in order to talk about the specialised products and services. At the same time, these topics must be dealt with in a positive manner – they are the bank's strengths. As a result, the texts contain a wide range of word groups combining nouns with positive adjectives.

Activity 5.10

Purpose: to extend your knowledge of the vocabulary used in more formal marketing communication.

Task: look at one or two web pages describing products for corporate customers. Identify the following examples of product benefits in the web pages:

- focusing on special products rather than everyday ones
- tailoring to the specific needs of the customer
- developing a relationship, rather than simply selling a one-off product
- emphasising the expertise of its people and teams
- demonstrating its track record and other credentials
- providing a long-term service
- showing the breadth of services provided.

Next, find some examples of noun groups consisting of adjectives + nouns used to talk about the bank's strengths. Create a table of strengths like the one below and write down the noun groups you find in the table. An example for each one is provided.

Strength	Adjective	Noun or noun group
special	imaginative	deal making
tailoring	bespoke	debt packages
relationship	consistent and supportive	presence
expertise	highly experienced	relationship managers
track record	huge	wealth of experience
service	value added	service
breadth	extensive	portfolio of investments
other (you define)		

There are no suggested answers for this activity as it is discussed in the comment below.

Comment

To some extent, these noun phrases give corporate banking communication a style that is similar to academic communication. The level of specialisation in this sector means that corporate banking departments and the companies they do business with are closer to universities in their activity than to the everyday mass market. This is reflected in the term **knowledge organisations**, which is often used to describe corporate banking departments or the companies they do business with. 'Knowledge' is the specialised expertise that these companies market. So it is not surprising that communication in this sector shares the style of academic communication. However, these are profit-making organisations and, although they may deal in knowledge, it is knowledge as a commodity. They are interested in selling what they produce. In their marketing documents, therefore, they look for a balance between the academic and the commercial.

The theme and point of the sentence

You saw earlier that the language used to address personal customers was direct; the grammatical subject of the verb was either missing – as in the use of imperatives – or it was *you*. In the more formal writing for marketing corporate banking, these forms are much less common.

Quite often, the name of the bank (or the specific department in question) becomes the subject of the sentence. Sometimes, *we* is used instead. Occasionally, the people from the bank become the subject. Finally, the strengths listed above can themselves become the subject (e.g. *Our experience* or *Our approach*).

As you might remember from previous sessions, the subject of a verb is usually also the theme of the sentence. This theme is what the sentence is about and the rest of the sentence makes a point about the theme. So in these formal marketing texts, by making the bank or its strengths the subject of sentences, the point of all the sentences can then be how the bank will make a positive difference for its corporate customers.

Activity 5.11

Purpose: to increase your awareness of typical subjects or themes used in formal marketing texts and how the rest of the sentence makes a positive point about these subjects.

Task 1: look through one or two web pages describing products for corporate customers. Prepare a table with the headings below. Copy a few sentences of each type indicated into the table. An example for each is provided.

Subject type	Subject/Theme	Point of the sentence
Name	The ... Bank	has an enviable reputation for imaginative deal making
We	We	offer a highly flexible approach
People	Experts in the key financial centres of Europe	complement our teams in London
Strength	Our depth of experience in the market	is unmatched
Other (you define)		

There are no suggested answers for this activity but it is discussed in the comment below.

Comment

The longer sentences of more formal marketing communication are necessary to allow the sentence to carry more information.

Levels of information in a sentence

Each of the example sentences above consists of a single **main clause**. This main clause can be followed by a list of products, services or activities as examples of what was in the main clause.

The table below shows several ways of achieving this. One is simply to add features using *with*. Another way is to use an *-ing* form. A third way is to combine an *-ing* form with another word, such as *with* or *while*. You can see examples of each of these in the table in the next activity.

Activity 5.12

Purpose: to increase your awareness of how phrases can be added to sentences in order to carry more detailed information.

Task: look at one or two web pages describing products for corporate customers. Create a table like the one below and copy a few sentences of each type indicated into the table (but be aware that you won't necessarily find all these types in one text).

Main clause	Connecting method	Added phrase
We offer extensive international coverage to our customers	**with**	with offices throughout Europe, North America and Asia.
Our experience covers a wide range of sectors	**-ing**	including manufacturing, agriculture and health care.
We use a hands-off approach to day-to-day operations of the business,	**with ... -ing** **while ... -ing**	while maintaining an active interest in the progress of our investments, in order to build category-leading organisations.

There are no suggested answers for this activity but it is discussed in the comment below.

Comment

These formal marketing sentences move between higher-level generalisations and lower-level details in the same way that you previously saw paragraphs in academic writing do. In addition, the way these sentences combine additional information with the main clause is similar to the way noun groups combine additional information with the main noun. The effect of both combinations is to produce texts which contain large amounts of information. This makes formal marketing texts different from personal banking texts, with their much smaller amounts of information, and more similar to the technical and formal academic texts you studied in Book 2.

The activities in this section so far should have given you insight into:

- the different approaches required to sell an organisation to different markets
- the different style of language used to do so.

Throughout this section, it should be apparent that the central idea behind the text is the customer. What are their wants, and what do they need to fulfil those wants? How does the product or service in question tie in with what they need?

One of the problems often experienced at work is that the people inside an organisation are all experts of one kind or another. They know a lot about the products they deal with or the work processes they are involved in. That is, of course, a good thing. The drawback, however, is that it is easy to become limited, thinking only about your field of specialist knowledge. This often means that, when dealing with the organisation's customers, it is very easy to forget to see the situation from the customer's point of view.

This was the issue with the text about 'Good Days Out' in Session 1 (Text 1.9), although it was written for an internal audience of the company and not its external market. The marketing specialists who wrote that text had a large amount of specialist knowledge about the consumer decision-making process and had to find ways to present this information to a less specialised audience. They had to adapt to their audience's different level of knowledge and different style of communicating.

In the next activity you will practise designing a text for a particular audience and, at the same time, revise what you have learned so far in this session.

Activity 5.13   ....

Purpose: to produce a marketing text for the corporate sector. To build your awareness of the need to tailor statements about products or services to the customer.

Task: think about the company website text you wrote in Activity 5.8. In that activity you wrote a marketing text for a mass market. In this activity you will prepare another marketing text, but this time for a specialised, corporate market. Work through the following steps.

Step 1

Decide whether the services or products of the company you imagined in Activity 5.8 can be aimed at a corporate business market. If they cannot, you will need to think of a new product or service which could be marketed to the corporate sector.

If you are working for, or have had experience of working for, a company, think about a small range of their products or services (don't try to cover everything); if the company focuses exclusively on the mass market, think creatively about what products or services could be of interest to the corporate niche. If you don't have any work experience, think about another organisation you know about (an educational organisation, or a club or society), and work creatively – what could the organisation offer to the business community?

(Again, you may find some of the suggestions for businesses in Text 5.4 in Resource Book 3 helpful in doing this.)

In the following steps you will build a text to market your chosen products or services. For each step, an example is given for an imaginary company providing corporate communication training. At times, it may be useful to refer back to the websites you looked at in Activities 5.9–5.12 and Online Activities 5.3 and 5.4 to see how a complete text like this looks.

Step 2

Make a list of one or more products or services your company can market.

Example: *corporate communication training*

Step 3

Quickly list who benefits from each item you listed above.

Example: *people engaged in international business*

Step 4

Write a sentence linking each product or service to the customer. Try to vary the sentence pattern and the verbs you use.

Example: *We provide our communication training services to a wide range of people engaged in international business.*

Step 5

Next to your list of customers, list what they want to do.

Example: *people engaged in international business*; *do business effectively in different countries.*

Step 6

Write a sentence linking the customers to specific wants.

Example: *As a person engaged in international business, you have to do business effectively.*

Step 7

Next to some of the wants, note down a need that will help the customer to achieve their want.

Example: *be able to speak English to a good standard.*

Step 8

Write some sentences linking the wants and the needs.

Example: *To be able to do business effectively, you need to speak English to a good standard.*

Step 9

Try to combine some or all of these elements (a customer, a want, a need, and a product or service) in one or two sentences. Then write another sentence, switching the elements around.

Example: *As a person engaged in international business, you want to do business effectively in different countries – and that means being able to speak English to a good standard. Our communication training services will help you to develop the skills to do this.*

Step 10

Make a list of a few features of your product, service or organisation.

Example: *tailor-made*

Step 11

Next to the features, make a note of the benefit that the customer gets from each feature.

Example: *tailor-made – the right language for your line of business.*

Step 12

Write sentences linking each feature to a benefit.

Example: *Because our communication training programmes are tailor-made, you can be sure that you will develop the right language for your line of business.*

Step 13

Write up your sentences as a text of about 500 words.

Step 14

Edit your text with reference to the Influential Document Checklist (see Appendix).

This is the end of the two sections on texts written about market services and products. You have now produced one fairly personal text for the mass market, and one which is more formal for the corporate market.

5.3 Finance documents

Describing financial data

Why figures?

Businesses are required to account for what they do. The accountants for small companies have to produce annual accounts for the owner, while larger businesses have to create annual reports. This information is used in a range of activities, including the definition of how much tax the organisation must pay, showing investors how the company is doing and allowing the organisation to control its spending, to measure its progress and to plan for the future. Consequently, all businesses produce figures.

Why write about figures?

Occasionally the figures speak for themselves and can be read simply by putting them in a table or in a diagram of some sort. So writing is not always necessary.

However, writing about figures becomes necessary for many reasons. The main reason is that writing text about figures can help the process of reading and understanding the significance of the figures. Text can quickly review the figures, presenting the relevant items to the reader in a slower – and therefore more readable – way. In other words, this kind of writing influences how the reader understands the figures.

Obviously, sales are of vital interest to any company. This is because sales provide income and, without income, there is no profit.

Larger corporations look at their sales from various points of view. For example, they may analyse them from the point of view of a particular division and the products or services they sell, or they may look at particular geographical markets and how they are performing.

Extract A is an example of a paragraph about sales from the report of a mobile phone company, published quarterly on the financial pages of the company's public website.

Extract A

Mobile Phones: First quarter 2006 net sales grew 30% to EUR 5.9 billion, compared with EUR 4.5 billion in the first quarter 2005, driven by strong industry volumes and our competitive product portfolio. Net sales increased in all regions year on year. Growth was strongest in North America, where our net sales more than doubled.

Writing basic sentences about sales figures

Here you will look at how to build up a paragraph like Extract A, describing a set of sales figures. You will start with simple sentences and the verbs used to state figures. You will then move on to look at how the paragraph can be organised. Later you will look at how other information can be included in the paragraph, the vocabulary that is used to describe figures, and the way different sets of information can be combined into single sentences.

Look at Table 5.1 which shows Nokia's sales of mobile devices. (*Mobile devices* include mobile phones but also other mobile technology such as hand-held computers.)

Table 5.1 Nokia mobile device volume by geographic area

(million units)	Q1 2006	Q1 2005	YoY change (%)	Q4 2005	QoQ change (%)
Europe	20.4	17.4	17	29.9	−32
Middle East and Africa	11.9	10.0	19	10.3	16
China	10.9	7.1	54	9.5	15
Asia-Pacific	16.4	10.6	55	14.8	11
North America	8.4	4.3	95	9.8	−14
Latin America	7.1	4.4	61	9.4	−24
Total	75.1	53.8	40	83.7	−10

(Source: www.nokia.com, 2007)

The figures show how many mobile devices were sold (in millions) in different geographical areas. These figures are primarily about the sales results for the first three months of 2006 (the first quarter of the year, or Q1), which are shown in the first column of figures (the second column from the left). Moving from left to right, the next column of figures shows the sales from the same quarter in the previous year. The third column of figures shows the change in the volume of sales from year to year (abbreviated to YoY). The fourth column shows the figures for the three months immediately before the current quarter, namely the last three months of 2005 (Q4 2005). The final column of figures shows the percentage change in sales from Q4 2005 to Q1 2006 (QoQ – or quarter on quarter). This quarter-on-quarter change is sometimes called the *sequential* increase or decrease.

Writing influentially about tables of figures like these requires precise, specific sentence patterns and particular vocabulary. As preparation for this kind of writing, you will practise these sentence patterns and vocabulary in the next activity. You are given the same model sentence and asked to write small variations on it. This activity is deliberately repetitive in order to reinforce the language patterns involved. However, you should move through the steps at your own pace, making your own decisions about how much repetition is useful for you. You may find you can miss out steps. If you decide to do this, make sure that you have noted the language pattern that is represented. It is a useful language learning activity to notice small differences between sentences which look similar at first sight.

Activity 5.14 ....

Purpose: to practise some basic sentence patterns for describing financial figures.

Task: work through the following steps, using the data in Table 5.1.

Step 1

Write three sentences that link the geographical area with the sales figure for Q1 2006.

Example and sentence pattern:

Sales in Europe	stood	at 20.4 million units in Q1 2006.
item	+ verb	+ figure

Use the sentence pattern above and the vocabulary alternatives suggested below.

Verbs: *amount to*, *stand at*, *total*, *reach*, *be*.

Step 2

Write three sentences that link the geographical area with the sales figure for Q1 2006.

Example and sentence pattern:

Nokia's European business	recorded	sales	of 20.4 million units in Q1 2006.
business area	+ verb	+ item	+ figure

Use the sentence pattern above and the vocabulary alternatives suggested below.

Verbs: *post*, *record*, *see*.

Step 3

Write three sentences that link the geographical area, the sales figure for Q1 2006, and the year-on-year growth percentage.

Example and sentence pattern:

Sales in Europe	stood	at 20.4 million units in Q1 2006,	up 17% on Q1 2005.
item	+ verb	+ figure	+ up/down + percentage + on + previous period

Step 4

Write three sentences that link the geographical area, the sales figure for Q1 2006, and the year-on-year growth percentage.

Example and sentence pattern:

Sales in Europe	stood	at 20.4 million units in Q1 2006,	an increase of 17% on Q1 2005.
item	+ verb	+ figure	+ trend noun + of + percentage + on + previous period

Use the sentence pattern indicated above and the vocabulary alternatives suggested below.

Trend nouns*: a rise, an increase, a fall, a decrease*.

Step 5

Write three sentences that link the geographical area and the year-on-year growth percentage.

Example and sentence pattern:

Sales in Europe	in Q1 2006	rose	by 17%	compared with Q1 2005.
item	+ period	+ trend verb	+ (by) + percentage	+ compared to + previous period

Use the sentence pattern indicated above and the vocabulary alternatives suggested below.

Trend verbs: *rise, increase, fall, decrease.*

Step 6

Write three sentences that link the geographical area, the year-on-year growth percentage and the actual figures.

Example and sentence pattern:

Sales in Europe	*rose*	*by 17%*	*from 17.4 million units in Q1 2005 to 20.4 million units in Q1 2006.*
item	+ trend verb	+ (by) + percent	+ from + figure + to + figure

Step 7

Write three sentences that link any of the items, but start your sentence with In + region.

Example and sentence pattern:

In Europe	*sales*	*rose*	*by 17%*	*from 17.4 million units in Q1 2005 to 20.4 million units in Q1 2006.*
in + region	item	+ trend verb	+ (by) + percent	+ from + figure + to + figure

Step 8

Write one sentence that joins any two of the sentences you have written previously.

Example and sentence pattern:

In Europe, sales rose by 17%, from 17.4 million units in Q1 2005 to 20.4 million units in Q1 2006,	*while*	*in China, sales rose by 54%, from 7.1 million units in Q1 2005 to 10.9 million units in Q1 2006.*
sentence 1	+ while	+ sentence 2

Comment

You should now be able to write several types of sentence describing sales figures. In the next activity, you will use them to write a full paragraph.

Activity 5.15

Purpose: to practise building up a paragraph about figures.

Task: write a paragraph that describes the sales figures in Table 5.1 comparing the figures for Q1 2006 and Q1 2005 for all the regions. Try to stick to one or two sentence patterns to make reading easy, but vary the vocabulary and the way you combine the information. Start the paragraph with a theme sentence which specifies the figures you are dealing with and which gives a high-level generalisation about their development (for example, *Sales of mobile units rose significantly throughout the world in Q1 2006*); end the paragraph with a statement of the total. Write a paragraph which could be published on the company's website.

Comment ....

When describing financial figures you need tight control of the types of sentence patterns you use so that a paragraph can be read quickly. However, it is useful to have a range of vocabulary alternatives available. The next activity aims to help you increase your vocabulary.

Writing about how figures change

There is a great variety of vocabulary for talking about how figures change – how they rise, how they fall and how they remain the same.

They can be divided into two main grammatical categories. The first category contains verbs which don't have objects – they just describe what happens to the subject. For example:

Sales rose.

Sales climbed to 17%.

(Verbs like this are called **intransitive verbs**.)

The second category contains verbs which must have objects – in other words, something is causing the change to something else. For example:

> *Sales boosted profits.*
>
> *The cost-cutting campaign reduced expenditure.*

(Verbs like this are called **transitive verbs**.)

Because transitive verbs have objects, it is possible to make passive sentences with them. For example:

> *Profits were boosted.*
>
> *Expenditure was reduced thanks to the cost-cutting campaign.*

Note that some verbs, such as *increase* and *decrease*, fall into both categories, for example:

Intransitive:	Sales increased.
Transitive:	The company increased its prices.
	Prices were increased.

Activity 5.16

Purpose: to build your vocabulary for describing change to figures.

Task: create tables with the headings below and write in some appropriate verbs. To help you do this, search the web for some company annual reports, i.e. the documents that a company publishes to present itself to the world. Skim through the sections on results or operating results. You could also find some articles from the business pages of a national newspaper. Remember that you can use a thesaurus to help you find alternative verbs to describe changes indicated by numbers.

Verbs for upward change

Intransitive verbs	Transitive verbs
rise	boost
increase	increase

Verbs for downward change

Intransitive verbs	Transitive verbs
fall	reduce
decrease	decrease

Ways to describe no change

be steady

There are no suggested answers for this activity because it is personal to you.

Comment   ....

To communicate precisely and interestingly about finance, it is useful to know a wide range of vocabulary and sentence patterns.

To focus on the language of financial change, next you will compare Nokia's sales figures for Q1 2006 with the figures for Q1 2007.

Activity 5.17   ....

Purpose: to read a short financial report.

Task: read Extract 5.5 in Resource Book 3, which is an extract from Nokia's report for 2007 Q1. Compare the figures with the previous set of figures which you looked at in Figure 5.1. Where is the company doing well, badly, or much the same?

Compare your answer with that suggested in the Answer section.

Comment   ....

The extract from Nokia's financial report covers much more than a simple description of the sales figures. It covers other aspects of the market such as market share. Significantly, it explains some of the changes in the markets.

Explaining financial change

Activity 5.18   ....

Purpose: to identify explanations in financial texts.

Task: look at Extract 5.5 in Resource Book 3 again and complete the table below. The left-hand column shows specific changes that have occurred. For each change, indicate what the cause is in the right-hand column.

Change	Cause
Nokia's year-on-year market share increase	
The lower year-on-year ASP (average sales price) in the first quarter	
ASPs for first quarter of 2007	
A significant ASP decline year on year	
The decrease in operating profit for the first quarter of 2007	

Compare your answers with those suggested in the Answer section.

Comment

Like all influential documents, international market reports have a specialised content and particular language patterns and vocabulary. However, the language of explanation in this activity is the same as you have studied earlier in this course. The next activity looks at this language of explanation more closely.

Activity 5.19

Purpose: to identify how explanations are signalled in text.

Task: fill in the middle column in the table below with the words that were used in Extract 5.5 to connect cause and effect.

Change	Connecting words	Cause
Nokia's year-on-year market share increase		strong gains in Asia-Pacific and Europe
The lower year-on-year ASP (average sales price) in the first quarter		a significantly higher proportion of entry-level device sales
ASPs for first quarter of 2007		a higher percentage of entry-level device sales.
A significant ASP decline year on year		a higher proportion of entry-level sales
The decrease in operating profit for the first quarter of 2007		lower sales of higher end, higher margin devices, and an increase in sales and marketing expenses

Compare your answers with those suggested in the Answer section.

Comment

Each explanation is connected to the change by means of a passive verb of cause – *drive*, *cause*, *impact* – or the verb *be (+ the result of).*

The following activity looks at other ways of linking cause and effect in financial writing.

Activity 5.20

Purpose: to practise some basic sentence patterns for explaining figures.

Task: use the information in the table below to construct sentences about Nokia's financial performance, connecting the change to the cause in the various ways described in each step.

As with Activity 5.14, there is a high level of repetition in this activity and you should adapt it to suit your own needs. If you decide you do not need to practise writing a particular sentence, notice what sentence pattern it demonstrates.

Change	Cause
Sales up	Growth in North America
Sales down	Competition in Central and South America
Costs up	Investments in new markets
Costs down	Results of cost-cutting campaign
Profit up	Growth in sales
Profit down	Slump in sales in Europe
Share price up	Improved performance across the board
Share price down	Lack of investor confidence in market expansion

Step 1

Write three sentences that state the change that has taken place and then link it to the cause.

Example and sentence pattern:

The rise in sales	*was triggered*	*largely by growth in North America.*
change	+ passive cause verb	+ cause

Use the sentence pattern above and the vocabulary suggested below.

Verbs: *be driven*, *be impacted*, *be caused*, *be triggered*, *be accounted for.*

Step 2

Write three sentences that state the change that has taken place and then link it to the cause.

Example and sentence pattern:

Sales rose significantly,	*triggered*	*largely by growth in North America.*
change	+ **past participle** of a passive cause verb	+ cause

Use the sentence pattern indicated above and the vocabulary suggested below.

Verbs: *be driven*, *be impacted*, *be caused*, *be triggered.*

Step 3

Write three sentences that state the change that has taken place and then link it to the cause.

Example and sentence pattern:

This rise in sales	*is principally attributable to*	*growth in North America.*
change	+ connecting effect words	+ cause

Use the sentence pattern indicated above and the vocabulary below.

Verbs: *reflect*, *be (in response to, a result of, attributable to)*, *result from, stem from.*

Step 4

Write three sentences that state the change that has taken place and then link it to the cause.

Example and sentence pattern:

This rise in sales	*was primarily due to*	*growth in North America.*
change	+ cause connectives	+ cause

Use the sentence pattern above and the vocabulary suggested below.

Cause connectives: *as a result of, due to, thanks to.*

Step 5

Write three sentences that state the cause and then link it to the change that has taken place.

Example and sentence pattern:

Growth in North America	*led to*	*a rise in sales overall.*
cause	+ cause verb	+ change

Use the sentence pattern above and the vocabulary suggested below.

Cause verbs: *drive, trigger, lead to, produce, affect, impact on, hit, helped, contributed to, account for.*

Step 6

Write three sentences that state the cause and then link it to the change that has taken place.

Example and sentence pattern:

Growth rose significantly in North America,	*contributing to*	*higher sales overall.*
cause	+ **present participle** of a cause verb	+ change

Use the sentence pattern above and the vocabulary suggested below.

Verbs: *driving, triggering, leading to, producing, impacting on, contributing to, accounting for.*

Step 7

Write three sets of two sentences. The first sentence should state the cause and the second sentence should state the change.

Example and sentence pattern:

Growth rose significantly in North America.	*As a result,*	*overall sales were better than expected.*
sentence 1	effect connective	+ sentence 2

Use the sentence pattern above and the vocabulary suggested below.

Effect connectives: *As a result, In response to this, Accordingly.*

Comment ....

You have practised a wide variety of explanation sentences. Your final task in this section is to write a short report describing a company's basic figures and giving explanations for the changes.

Activity 5.21 ....

Purpose: to write a short report describing and explaining a company's performance for the company's public website.

Task 1: look at the figures in Table 5.2. Make notes on:

(a) How this company is doing overall.

(b) Which item has the most impact on the overall result.

(c) Who are the strong performers in sales, and who are the weak performers.

(d) What effect costs have on the overall result.

(e) What are the successes and concerns in terms of costs.

Table 5.2   Financial data for a company

	Area	*2006 (US$ million)*	*2005 (US$ million)*	*Change (%)*
	Rest of the world	10	10	0
Sales	China	05	03	66
	Total	15	13	15
	Rest of the world	06	07	−14
Costs	China	04	03	66
	Total	10	10	0
Profit		05	03	66

Task 2: when you have made your notes, design a short report describing and explaining the figures. Give your text a title and give strong theme sentences to the paragraphs, stating what the paragraphs are about at a high level of generalisation. Use the sentence patterns and vocabulary you have studied in this session.

5.4 Conclusion

The documents that companies produce to present themselves to the outside world are an important factor in their success. Through these texts, companies communicate with their customers and partners and create a dialogue and a relationship.

The marketing and finance texts you have looked at in this session, unlike the essays you write for a business studies course, are written for audiences of many people and, as a result, are often produced by many writers. The skills of these individual writers are developed through the experience of tailoring their writing style to varied purposes and audiences. Selling your knowledge to a tutor in terms that will persuade the tutor to accept it is different from selling company knowledge to a corporate market, or services to a mass market. However, in all these cases you have to: understand the needs and wants of the audience; choose the organisation of the text and the style of language appropriately; and recognise what the audience knows and doesn't know. It is through their skill in carrying out these processes that writers produce influential documents.

5.5 Review

In this session you should have:

- developed your skills and language for writing short marketing documents
- developed your vocabulary for writing about personal and corporate banking
- developed your skills and language for writing about finance
- written two marketing documents and a finance document.

5.6 Answer section

Activity 5.1

Good workplace documents should be:

• correct and sufficient in the information they provide	A
• clearly focused on a specific purpose	B
• clearly focused on the user of the document	C
• well-organised and well-thought through	B, E
• readable and concise	B, E
• presentable in layout and accurate in writing	F

Activity 5.5

Tasks 1 and 2

Additional examples from Text 5.1 are in italics.

Sentence pattern	Examples
Vocabulary – benefit verbs	The monthly mortgage repayment calculator **will help** you work our your repayments *you'll save 10% off the latest cost of your holiday* *receive a £50 bonus discount* *make fantastic savings* *our exclusive offer gives you up to 50% off the brochure price*
Can	With our ..., **you can get** a great package of benefits. *you can take advantage of savings* *you can forget the timetables of conventional cruises*
Offers	The bank's card **offers you** a fantastic rate of interest.
Promises	**We'll send you** a monthly statement. *you are guaranteed expert travel advice* *you'll save 10% off the latest cost of your holiday*
Noun phrases	**No repayments** for three months *the best availability* *a £50 bonus discount* *our exclusive offer* *£100 per couple bonus discount* *fantastic savings*
Imperatives	**Get** 5.5% with our instant access savings account. *get booking now* *Choose from New York, Boston ...*
Introductory phrases and clauses	**Whether you're new to investments, or an existing customer**, you will find ... *So whether you're looking for a last-minute bargain ...* *get booking now*

Activity 5.6

Task 1

Examples from Texts 5.2 and 5.3.

Verb type	Examples
Benefits	help you, allow you to, you can
Guarantee	we guarantee
Importance/need	you need to know
Offer/reassurance	we'll be pleased to, we'll back it up with

Adjective type	Examples
Specialness	special, fantastic
Speed	quick, more than fast, automated
Ease	easy, simple
Availability	available

Adverb type	Examples
Ease of use	just

Other phrases – type	Examples
Cheapness	it doesn't have to cost you a penny, all you pay
Reassurance	peace of mind, no problem
Convenience	at your finger tips, any time of day, whenever you want, added convenience, any time from, how's that for convenience?
Speed	as soon as they arrive, in three hours

Activity 5.7

Task 1

Text 5.2	Text 5.3
Paragraph 1: Customer's needs – Benefits of the product	Paragraph 1: Need – Benefit – Offer
Paragraph 2: Need – Benefit. Benefit. Need – Benefit	Paragraph 2: Offer
Paragraph 3: Benefits	Paragraph 3: Benefits
Paragraph 4: How to obtain	Paragraph 4: Reassurance
	Paragraphs 5 and 6: How to obtain

Task 2

Texts 5.2 and 5.3

A quotation from a customer at the beginning

Incomplete sentences without verbs, or without pronoun subjects

Short sentences

And as a connective at the beginning of sentences

Personal pronouns: *you, your, our, us, we*

Question and answer

Short forms: *we'll, that's, doesn't*

Conversational words: *OK, stuck, bang up to date, give us a call, sort out bills, fiendish*

Here-and-now instructions: *do it now, please give us a call*

Activity 5.9

- Focusing on special products rather than everyday ones.
- Tailoring to the specific needs of the customer.
- Developing a relationship, rather than simply selling a one-off product.
- Emphasising the expertise of the bank's people and teams.
- Demonstrating its track record and other credentials.
- Providing a long-term service.
- Showing the breadth of services provided.

Activity 5.17

As Extract 5.5 states in various places, the company is doing well in Europe and Asia, and poorly in North America.

Activity 5.18

Change	Cause
Nokia's year-on-year market share increase	Strong gains in Asia-Pacific and Europe
The lower year-on-year ASP (average sales price) in the first quarter	A significantly higher proportion of entry-level device sales
ASPs for first quarter of 2007	A higher percentage of entry-level device sales
A significant ASP decline year on year	A higher proportion of entry-level sales
The decrease in operating profit for the first quarter of 2007	Lower sales of higher end, higher margin devices, and an increase in sales and marketing expenses

Activity 5.19

Change	Connecting words	Cause
Nokia's year-on-year market share increase	**was driven primarily by**	strong gains in Asia-Pacific and Europe
The lower year-on-year ASP (average sales price) in the first quarter	**was primarily the result of**	a significantly higher proportion of entry-level device sales
ASPs in first quarter of 2007	**were impacted by**	a higher percentage of entry-level device sales
A significant ASP decline year on year	**Was driven primarily by**	a higher proportion of entry-level sales
The decrease in operating profit for the first quarter of 2007	**was primarily caused by**	lower sales of higher end, higher margin devices, and an increase in sales and marketing expenses

SESSION 6 Writing workplace proposals

6.1 Introduction

By now, you should be familiar with techniques for describing various business scenarios and examining them critically, giving reasons for your arguments and predicting the reactions of other people to the ideas you put forward.

In this session you will examine another type of influential document: the workplace proposal. The aim is to equip you with the tools to analyse a situation, consider ways in which it could be improved on, and produce a document with the power to convince other people of the effectiveness of what you propose. You will learn what is involved in writing workplace proposals in terms of what to include, how to present the information and how to use language effectively.

Learning outcomes

In this session you will:

- gain an understanding of the function of workplace proposals
- increase your knowledge of the features of workplace proposals
- learn to analyse situations in terms of problems and solutions
- familiarise yourself with the possible structures of workplace proposals
- develop the language that makes them effective
- apply your own knowledge and skills by writing your own workplace proposal.

6.2 What is a workplace proposal?

You will begin by considering what distinguishes workplace proposals from the other influential documents that you have encountered in this book. In broad terms, workplace proposals are concerned with recommending **solutions** to work-based **problems**.

Activity 6.1

Purpose: to consider potential solutions to workplace problems.

Task: match the six problems below with the proposed solutions.

Problem	Possible solution
1 In order to meet the requirements of corporate social responsibility, a company is seeking ways in which to implement more ecological approaches to the use of resources.	A The company should investigate the possibility of developing and/or manufacturing different products, building on existing expertise and plant.
2 A hitherto successful chain of retail men's clothing outlets has found that their sales are declining to the point where they may need to close stores in some areas.	B The company could research the particular customer groups in the different areas where their stores are located and the products are likely to be in demand.
3 Staff turnover in a company has increased beyond acceptable levels and there are indicators that this may be due to a high level of dissatisfaction with working conditions.	C The company ought to introduce more flexible hours, including late night or Sunday opening, compensated for by closing in quieter periods.
4 Technological development has resulted in a severe decline in demand for what was the most popular product of a small manufacturing company.	D The company could consider a range of ecological strategies, including energy-saving policies, recycling systems, structural changes to buildings and incentives to employees to use public transport or bicycles.
5 A multinational supermarket has found that competitors are outstripping it in certain geographical areas because of the broader range of goods on offer, particularly catering to the requirements of certain groups.	E The company should do a market research exercise to find out what customers want, and eventually introduce a more versatile range of products.
6 A small retail outlet has found that there are times of day and days of the week when business is very slow, and others which are very busy. They are not sure if their hours are catering for the maximum number of customers.	F The company needs to consider ways of establishing employer–employee communication with the aim of understanding and eventually meeting the need for acceptable working conditions.

Compare your answers with those suggested in the Answer section.

Comment

The focus here is on suggesting ways of addressing problems which have yet to be resolved. Proposals therefore look ahead to *future* action.

Activity 6.2 ....

Purpose: to familiarise yourself with the purpose of a workplace proposal.

Task: consider the following work-related problem. How would you solve it? Write your solution in the box below.

Problem

A member of staff in a workplace team is behaving in a way which is alienating other members of the team and disrupting the smooth running of the work on a day-to-day basis. The person is very good at their job (particularly with customers) and achieves their targets but there have been many complaints from colleagues about their hostile attitude to fellow members of the team, and inappropriate comments and remarks. The team leader has referred the situation to the Human Resources department.

Suggested solution

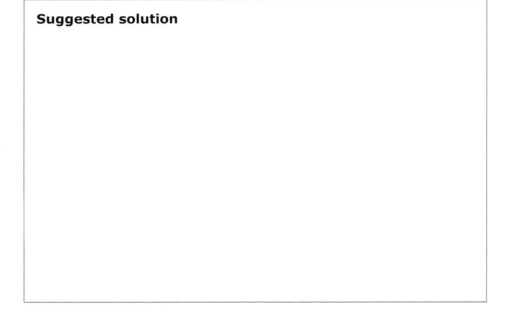

Comment ....

By suggesting a possible solution to this workplace problem, you have effectively made a proposal.

The purpose of workplace proposals

Workplace proposals can be defined as problem-solving documents in that they attempt to persuade another party to take some form of **action** in order to achieve a specific, beneficial **goal**. In many proposals the action is likely to be the same as the solution to the problem. However, in some proposals, solution and action may be separated, the action being the **steps** towards the solution. The actions that are proposed may be either **internal** – such as recommending a new way of doing something within a company – or **external** – such as convincing a funding body to commit resources to a particular cause or purpose.

Persuasiveness

Note the different verbs that are used to describe the purposes of proposals in the above definition, among them *persuade ...*, *recommend ...* and *convince ...* Which other verbs could you add to this list? (Some examples are given after Activity 6.1 in the Answer section.)

You could argue that all influential documents aim to be persuasive in some way. What distinguishes business proposals from other persuasive documents is that they attempt to convince other people of the validity of your suggested solution to a problem, and to persuade them to take the necessary action to implement it.

Goals

This next activity takes a closer look at the notion of **goals** in relation to proposals. Goals are the benefits you aim to achieve by taking a proposed line of action to address a particular problem. The goal of the proposed action in scenario 1 of Activity 6.1 is most likely to be reducing the company's environmental impact. A linked goal might be lowering company expenditure. What might be the goals of the other five scenarios?

Activity 6.3

Purpose: to become familiar with the concept of goals in relation to proposals.

Task: look again at scenarios 2 to 6 in Activity 6.1. For each one, write down what you think the intended goal might be.

Compare your answers with those suggested in the Answer section.

Comment

Achieving a goal is the purpose of the proposal and there would be no proposal without one. The language for writing about goals is studied later in this session.

The functions of workplace proposals

This section introduces a range of **functions** that can be found in workplace proposals. These functions are listed in Table 6.1 in the order in which they commonly occur in a proposal text. Use the list as a point of reference as you work through the session. It is important to bear in mind, however, that proposal texts do not follow a formula. Not only may the sequencing vary but also some functions are optional, while others may include several possible sub-functions.

Table 6.1   The functions of workplace proposals

	Function	*Description*
1	Problem description	Identifying problem
		Establishing cause(s) and effect(s)
2	Statement of goals	
3	Solution statement	Proposing solution
		Making recommendations
		Describing solution
		(Action required to implement it; internal or external action; steps in action; goals of action)
		Making pre-emptive responses to predicted objections
		(Reservations, argument and response, counter-argument, thinking about the reader)
4	Benefits statement	
5	Call to action	

Next you will read an extract of a workplace proposal and identify the main functions that you have met so far.

Activity 6.4   ....

Purpose: to identify the functions in a workplace proposal.

Task: read through Text 6.1 in Resource Book 3 once. Then read it again and identify and label the sections corresponding to:

(a) the problem (P)

(b) what the writer considers to be the beneficial goal (G)

(c) the solution that is being proposed (S)

(d) whether the action is internal (I) or external (E).

Compare your answers with those suggested in the Answer section.

Comment   ....

There are more functions in Text 6.1 which you will consider as you work through later activities.

6.3 Writing a workplace proposal

The activities in this section practise writing proposals with the functions you have identified. You will do this by writing about scenarios from your workplace or a similar environment. Because each activity builds on the previous one, it is important that you work through them in turn and save your work as you go in MyStuff.

Note that, because many of the writing tasks involve drawing on your own ideas, suggested answers are not always provided in the Answer section.

Describing a problem

Activity 6.5 ···

Purpose: to identify a set of problems in a particular environment or situation.

Task: using your word processor, create a table with the headings below, in landscape format.

In Session 2 you wrote a description of a current or past work environment or an organisation you are familiar with (this could include your home environment).

In your table, list up to three things that you would like to see changed or that you think could be improved within that environment or organisation. The items on your list do not have to be in any particular order.

You will refer back to this table as you work through the activities in this session.

Problem item	Description
1	
2	
3	

Comment ···

As you should recall from Book 1, it is helpful to 'unpack' problems to establish their **cause(s)** and their **effect(s)**. Flow diagrams can provide clear representations of this, as in Figures 6.1 and 6.2.

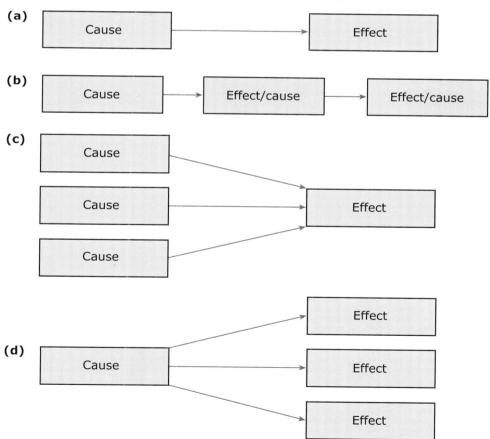

Figure 6.1 Flow diagrams of different types of cause–effect relationships: (a) type 1; (b) type 2; (c) type 3; (d) type 4

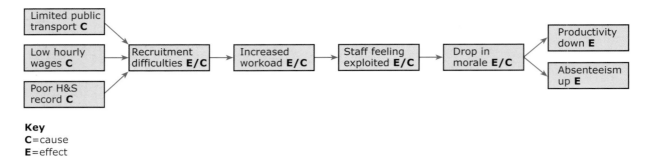

Key
C=cause
E=effect

Figure 6.2   Cause–effect relationships applied to a particular problem scenario or text

You will use cause–effect analysis like this in the next activity.

Activity 6.6   ....

Purpose: to analyse the cause and effect elements of problems.

Task: look again at the problems you listed in Activity 6.5. Take each problem in turn and unpack it in the form of a flow diagram, indicating what you consider to be the cause(s) and the effect(s) of each one.

There is no suggested answer for this activity but it is discussed in the comment below.

Comment   ....

Analysing the cause and effect elements of problems is likely to form part of writing workplace proposals. It can indicate which goal or goals should be pursued in order to solve the problem, which steps are likely to solve the problem, the benefits that are likely to result, and which arguments against the proposal the writer will need to find responses to. These uses of cause–effect analysis are considered in the activities which follow.

Writing a problem description for a proposal

A **problem description** is a key feature of a written proposal. Next you will see how a reference to cause and effect is likely to form part of this description.

Activity 6.7   ....

Purpose: to compare two ways of describing the same work-based problem and to see how text structure, the language of the reader–writer relationship, and the language of text organisation can be used to create an influential problem analysis (see Sections B, D and E of the Influential Document Checklist).

Task: Extracts A and B below are two descriptions of the same work-based problem. Read them both carefully and then do the following.

(a) Draw a flow chart for each text identifying what seem to be the cause(s) and the effect(s) of the problem.

(b) Note down at least three differences between the two texts in terms of their written style. Try to identify at least one feature from Sections D and E of the Influential Document Checklist.

There is no suggested answer for this activity but feedback is given in the comment below.

Extract A

I've noticed that there are an awful lot of cigarette butts lying around outside the main door to the office. I think something should be done about it because it looks very messy. On top of that, there always seems to be someone hanging around there having a fag and getting in the way. Something should be done about it.

Extract B

Following the introduction of the smoking ban, it has become a frequent occurrence for some staff to congregate outside the main entrance to the building to smoke. This can impede access to the building, and the resulting discarded cigarette butts are unsightly and create an unattractive impression for visitors. This situation needs to be resolved.

Comment

In considering the differences between the styles of the two texts, you probably established that Extract B is a more successful example of a problem description than Extract A. What makes it so? Sections of the Influential Documents Checklist will be used as the basis for comparing the texts, starting with Section B, *The organisation of the text*.

Extract A is not very clearly structured in terms of the organisation of its content. An unnecessarily repeated sentence contributes to this lack of clarity:

Something should be done about it

In contrast, the organisation and sequencing of Extract B is clearer and more logical, making it much easier to follow.

The difference in the quality of organisation of Extracts A and B is also reflected in the language used for this purpose. This is the focus of Section E of the checklist, *The language of text organisation*.

Thus, in Extract A, language is not used as effectively as it could be to support the organisation of the text. In order to describe the cause–effect basis of the problem, it is helpful if the themes of each sentence are linked with the sentence(s) before and if cause–effect connectives are used. In fact, the themes of two sentences in Extract A are linked with the sentences before by repeating the pronoun *I* (*I've noticed* and *I think*). Focusing on *I* takes attention away from the problem being described. The other sentence is linked by the pronoun *that* in *On top of that* which does make a link to the problem situation in the previous sentence, but the connective *On top of* is not a cause effect connective. The result is that it is not easy to establish what the causes are and what the effects of the problem being described are.

In Extract B, the sequencing of the theme and the point of each sentence are much clearer, with themes, links and connectives contributing to the overall coherence of the text. This makes it much easier to identify the **causes** of the problem:

Theme

> *Following the introduction of the smoking ban*

Point

> *staff congregating to smoke outside the main entrance*

and the **effects**:

Theme

> *This*

Point

> *impedes access to the building*

Theme

> *and the resulting discarded cigarette butts*

Point

> *are unsightly and create an unattractive impression*

Section D of the Influential Document Checklist is concerned with the extent to which the language used in a document creates an appropriate relationship between reader and writer.

Extract A appears to have a different anticipated audience from Extract B. This is reflected first in its informal style, similar to that of casual speech, as manifested in the many colloquial expressions it contains:

on top of that, an awful lot of, lying around, hanging around, having a fag, getting in the way.

This kind of informality introduces an emotional and casual quality into the text which is generally regarded as unsuitable for written proposals and is likely to reduce the effectiveness of the document.

The problem is described from a personal, subjective perspective, through the use of expressions such as: *I've noticed ..., I think ...*

This suggests that the writer is not specifically focused on proposing action for the problem, but simply giving their opinion. In general, personalised statements such as these are best avoided when building a relationship with the likely audience of a workplace proposal.

The language of Extract B is more effective in creating an effective reader–writer relationship for a written proposal.

First, it uses a more formal range of language:

staff, congregate, discarded cigarette butts, create an unattractive impression

Second, the problem is described more objectively. Instead of referring to their views, as is the case in Extract A, the writer of Extract B uses impersonal constructions such as:

This can impede access ...

This has the effect of focusing the reader's attention on the cause–effect aspects of the problem rather than on the views of the writer. It is worth bearing in mind that, if the writer is in a position of authority, an emotional or evaluative subjective style can be considered threatening. If the writer is not in a position of authority, this emotional, personal style can be seen as confrontational or simply lacking in seriousness. Therefore, an effective proposal is likely to avoid expressions which bring the writer's personality to the reader's attention.

Next you will practise writing a problem description in the style of Extract B.

Activity 6.8

....

Purpose: to practise writing a problem description in an effective style.

Task: choose one of the problems you listed in Activity 6.5. Write a paragraph (150–200 words) describing the problem, basing your writing on the features of Extract B with respect to the organisation of the text, the organisational language and the language of the reader–writer relationship.

Writing a statement of goals for a workplace proposal

In order to propose a solution for the problems identified in a situation, the proposer must have a goal in mind. The goal is the desired state; the situation when the problem is solved. In some respects, without a goal, there is no problem. Unless the proposer can imagine a desired, different state, there is no reason to be dissatisfied with the current situation. The goal is what is wanted. The solution is what is needed to achieve the goal. In this section, you will look at how to write **a statement of goals**.

Activity 6.9

....

Purpose: to identify some goals for a set of problematic situations.

Task 1: revise what goal statements are like by re-reading the part of Text 6.1 in Resource Book 3 which states the goal of the proposal. Remember that there is a *general* goal statement and a *specific* goal statement. Then look at the preface of Text 6.2, which is another proposal, and underline the general goal statement. Note that, whereas problem statements refer to present or past time, goal statements usually refer to future time in some way.

Task 2: create a second column in your table of problems from Activity 6.5 and label it 'Goal'. In this column note down which goal you would like to achieve by addressing each problem you have listed.

Problem item	Goal
1	
2	
3	

Task 3: add a goal statement to the proposal you wrote in Activity 6.8.

Compare your answers with those suggested in the Answer section.

Comment ....

The information in your table provides the reason for writing a proposal. It consists of a present, undesirable problem and a future, desirable goal. The purpose of the proposal is to show how to reach the goal.

Proposing a solution

So far, you have focused on the problem description and the goal statement of a written proposal. In this section you will look at the solution statement. This is the main point of the proposal: a document would not be a proposal without it.

The solution statement is made up of several elements (see Figure 6.1). In these activities they will be treated separately, although it will be obvious that in the text examples, they are integrated in various ways.

Now you will look at another extract of text. This one describes a work-based problem and proposes a possible solution.

Activity 6.10 ....

Purpose: to note the features of a problem–solution text in a written proposal.

Task: read Extract C below and then answer the following questions.

(a) What is the problem? Underline and label it (P).

(b) What are the cause(s) and effect(s) of the problem being described?

(c) Underline and label them (C) and (E).

(d) What is the goal? Underline and label it (G).

(e) What is the proposed solution? Underline and label it (S).

> ### Extract C
>
> It is now becoming more frequent for businesses to have plans to put into action in the event of disasters such as fire, flood, disease and terrorism. Our organisation currently lacks such a disaster plan. This has several potential implications. First, it means the organisation has not taken every care for the safety and security of our staff who may suffer injury or death as a result of the organisation's lack of planning. Second, it means the organisation runs the risk of being severely disrupted as a result of an occurrence of this kind. Third, it means that the organisation could be held responsible for any deaths and injuries arising from such an event. Finally, it means that the organisation may already be losing business, if client companies are not confident of our ability to continue trading in the wake of a disaster. In order to address these concerns, it is recommended that a disaster plan be produced with some urgency.

Compare your answer with that suggested in the Answer section.

Comment ....

Extract C contains a description of a problem, a cause–effect analysis and the proposed solution. It does not have an explicit statement of the goal.

Several points can be made about the use of language in Extract C.

First, the paragraph contains a **list**. Lists are common in proposal documents. This list is a list of the effects in the cause–effect analysis of the problem. Text 6.1 contains a list used for a different purpose. This list is examined later in this section but you should look briefly at Text 6.1 now to identify the list and what its purpose is.

Lists were first introduced in the staff restaurant report in Session 1 of this book. Note the following features associated with incorporating a list in a written text.

- A phrase is used to introduce the list. In Extract C, it is:

This has several potential implications ...

- Each item is presented in turn by a sequencing word or expression. In this case they are:

  First, ...

  Second, ...

  Third, ...

  Finally, ...

- The phrases presenting each item in the list are grammatically parallel, as in the following structure:

  It means that the organisation [+ problem]

The second feature of interest in Extract C is the statement of recommendation which is used to propose the solution.

You have already encountered several examples of the language used in making statements of recommendation in the texts you have read so far. These are examined further in the next activity.

Activity 6.11 ....

Purpose: to decide on suitable words for making recommendations.

Task 1: read the four statements of recommendation below. Identify the statement that was used in Extract C and decide why the writer chose to use it and not one of the other statements.

(a) The committee	should	produce	a disaster plan.

(b) A disaster plan	should	be	produced.

(c) I	recommend	that	the committee	produce	a disaster plan.

(d) It is	recommended	that	a disaster plan	be	produced.

Task 2: Extract D below is the recommendation section of the staff restaurant report from Session 1. Which of the four recommendation statements above is closest to the recommendation statement in Extract D?

Extract D

RECOMMENDATIONS

In order to rectify the unsatisfactory situation summarised in Section D, the Working Party recommends that urgent consideration be given to implementing the following measures:

1   two lunch sittings should be introduced
2   the quality of food and choice of dishes must be improved
3   the kitchen should be re-equipped with cost-reducing equipment
4   a second user queue to a second cash register should be introduced.

Compare your answers with those suggested in the Answer section.

Comment

The four statements of recommendation show how impersonal language is used in proposals to make it easier for the audience to judge the proposal without entering into a direct relationship with the writer. It is more important for the proposal to be persuasively organised than to be written in a forceful language style. The next activity focuses on this.

Activity 6.12

Purpose: to see how the functions **problem identification**, **goal statement** and **recommendation** are organised into a proposal text.

Task: read Extract E below. Then underline and label the sentences that correspond to:

(a) the problem (P)

(b) the cause(s) and effect(s) analysis of the problem (C and E)

(c) the goal (G)

(d) the recommended solution (S).

Which structure has been used in the solution statement?

> **Extract E**
>
> On several occasions, it has been unclear whether or not a specific document has in fact been sent out to our clients. This has sometimes led to embarrassment and could jeopardise our long-term relationship with them. It also means that considerable time and energy are spent in tracking the document in question. It is important that all our documents can be tracked efficiently so that this kind of uncertainty does not occur in future. It is therefore recommended that a document log be created for this purpose.

Compare your answers with those suggested in the Answer section.

Comment

Extract E embeds a statement about goals between the problem description and the solution statement. As mentioned earlier, goals are what you aim to achieve in addressing a particular problem and implementing a solution.

Activity 6.13

Purpose: to identify some possible solutions to a set of problems.

Task: create a third column in your table from Activity 6.9 and label it 'Solution', as shown below.

For each of the three problems that you listed earlier, think of a possible solution and note it in the 'Solution' column.

Problem item	Goal	Solution
1		
2		
3		

Comment ....

You will need to refer back to this table in later activities.

Activity 6.14 ....

Purpose: to practise linking a problem description with a solution statement.

Task: using Extracts C and D as models, select two of the problem–goal–solution sets that you listed in Activity 6.13 and write one or two paragraphs for each, linking the three elements. Where possible, include a list indicating the cause(s) and/or effect(s) of the problem.

Your statement of recommendation should be based on one of the language structures outlined above.

Comment ....

At the end of this session you will incorporate this writing into a complete proposal.

Writing about the steps in the action proposed

A solution is a proposal for action and an influential proposal is likely to explain the steps in the action. The solution that you studied in Book 1, Session 5, is a good example of this. In response to criticisms of working conditions at Gap's manufacturers, a recommended solution was *partnership sourcing*. But, to persuade the company to implement this solution, the proposal included a description of how partnership sourcing could be carried out as well as the benefits that would follow.

This section focuses on the steps in the action. Outlining the steps in the action is often combined with describing goals or benefits.

Activity 6.15 ··

Purpose: to note how the action is described and explained in a few proposals.

Task 1: look again at Text 6.1. You identified the action in this proposal in Activity 6.4. Look again at the action. Identify the steps and what other information is included, in addition to the description of the action step itself.

Compare your answer with the one in the Answer section before you move on.

Task 2: read Text 6.2 in Resource Book 3, which is a proposal for reorganising a department in a store. There are descriptions of the action involved in Recommendations 2 and 4. Identify the number of steps involved in each recommendation.

Compare your answers with those suggested in the Answer section.

Comment ··

The steps in the action are not always as clearly laid out as they are in Text 6.1. Text 6.2 is a more detailed proposal and so the steps are not presented in a list as they are in Text 6.1. In fact, it would be possible to organise the steps in Text 6.2 more clearly by using the introductory words *the first*, *the second*, *the third step* and more parallel grammar in each of the steps.

The steps in both texts are combined with the goal or benefit that will be obtained by carrying out the step. In Text 6.1, this is expressed in a simple way at the end of each step. In Text 6.2, the benefits are also very obviously stated but in more detail.

Activity 6.16 ··

Purpose: to identify what steps are needed to implement the solution to a problem.

Task: create a fourth column on the right-hand side of your table from Activity 6.13. In this column note down the steps or action required to implement the solution.

Problem item	Goal	Solution	Steps or action
1			
2			
3			

Writing a benefits statement

Goals and benefits are connected. The purpose of the proposal is to demonstrate how the solution that is proposed will move the organisation from a situation perceived as a problem towards a more desired state – the goal. The desirability of the goal may be obvious, but it may be more persuasive to emphasise why it is desirable by explaining the benefits of the solution proposed. The purpose of benefits statements is to underline the reasons for the proposed action and the positive outcomes that will ensue as a result of this.

Benefit statements can refer to the entire proposal, as in the example from Text 6.1 below. Extract F is the benefits statement. If you compare Extract F with the goal statement in Extract G, you can see how the benefits statement is similar to the goal statement. You can also see that one of the differences is that the benefits statement emphasises the positive value of achieving the goal more strongly.

Extract F

We are convinced that the proposed action will provide the department with the necessary information on which to base further action to remedy the problem of absenteeism from training programmes.

Extract G

In order to address this [problem], we first need to know what the true level of attendance is and what factors contribute to non-attendance.

Extract F uses positive evaluation words – *convinced*, *necessary* and *remedy* – to describe the impact of achieving the goal which is described in more neutral words in Extract G. By emphasising the positive impact of the solution, the writer is using the *strength* concept from the SWOT (Strengths, Weaknesses, Opportunities, Threats) framework to analyse the future condition of the organisation. In the next activity you will use SWOT analysis to frame your reading of the conclusion of Text 6.2.

Activity 6.17

Purpose: to identify the positive words used to describe the benefits of a proposed solution.

Task: read the Conclusion of Text 6.2 for an overview of what it is about. Then read it again, using the concepts from the SWOT analysis to frame your reading. Identify the negative evaluation words used to describe the Threat; the positive evaluation words used to describe the Opportunity; the negative evaluation words used to describe the Weaknesses; and the positive evaluation words which describe the benefits of carrying out the proposal in order to move the organisation into a position of Strength.

Compare your answers with those suggested in the Answer section.

Comment

The Conclusion of Text 6.2 begins with a description of the current sales environment as both a threat and an opportunity, points out the weakness of the organisation's current response to this opportunity, and encourages the organisation to consider the proposed solution in terms of the benefits it will bring the organisation. In other words, the proposal will put the organisation back into a desired position of strength. In the Conclusion, the emphasis is on the benefits of the proposal; the majority of the evaluation words deal with these benefits.

As you saw in Activity 6.15, each step in the proposed action can have a goal statement attached. Often these goal statements are expressed with a high level of positive evaluation and in effect become benefits statements. It would be normal for these to accumulate into the overall benefit statements. Look back at the goal statements attached to each step in Texts 6.1 and 6.2 and identify how much positive evaluation is used. Are these goal statements also benefit statements?

Writing a call to action

Now you will look at how the authors of Texts 6.1 and 6.2 in Resource Book 3 compose a call to action, a statement that is designed to provoke the reader(s) to act.

The final sentence of Text 6.1 is the call to action:

We recommend it to the Management Team for approval.

Its purpose is to end the proposal by emphasising what the document is for. The function of a proposal is to be accepted by its reader(s). None of the solutions, actions and benefits in the document will occur if its readers do not decide to accept the proposal. The call to action puts that fact clearly at the end of the document.

The call to action in Text 6.1 is very direct. The management team can have no doubt about what is expected of them. The call to action in the Staff Restaurant Report is equally direct:

In order to rectify the unsatisfactory situation summarised in Section D, the Working Party recommends that urgent consideration be given to implementing the following measures: ...

Other direct calls to action include:

I or we urge the Board of Directors to consider this proposal seriously.

We strongly recommend that this recommendation be ...

I or we trust that you will look on this proposal favourably ...

However, calls to action may be less direct. Text 6.2 does not contain a direct call to action.

Activity 6.18

....

Purpose: to study an indirect call to action.

Task: Text 6.2 in Resource Book 3 does not end with a direct call to action. Study the Conclusion of Text 6.2 and decide how the writer calls the reader(s) to action.

Compare your answer with that suggested in the Answer section.

Comment

....

Both benefits statements and calls to action are direct communications with the audience and, in these parts of the proposal, the interaction with the reader is obvious. However, interaction with readers goes on all through proposal documents – more or less obviously. The next section looks at how this is done.

Engaging with the reader

As you saw above, workplace proposals are problem-solving documents. Yet, over and above this, they are persuasive documents. The next few activities explore the notion of persuasiveness further.

As mentioned earlier, proposals require some kind of action. This entails the use of time, effort, money and other resources – all of which are in limited supply. The expectation therefore is that people reading the proposal will evaluate it critically. Among the questions they might ask themselves are whether the proposed action represents a good use of their limited resources and what the effect will be if the proposal is ignored.

The first implication for you as the writer of the proposal is to find out as much as possible about its prospective readers.

If the proposal is for internal purposes, such as recommending a new way of doing something within the company, you will need to approach the people in your organisation who know the prospective audience and can anticipate how they are likely to react.

If the proposal is for external purposes (for example, to sell a service to a potential client), you need to read all the relevant information available about that client, communicate with them directly, and engage with those people in your organisation who know about them. These contacts and enquiries will provide valuable information on the factors likely to come into play in the reader's evaluation of your proposal.

Now read Extract H below, which is from a proposal.

Extract H

During recent annual staff appraisal meetings, the majority of my team members requested training in the use of Microsoft Excel. This is proving a useful tool in planning their current design project. Yet on the occasions that they are required to use this program, it is clear that many team members are unfamiliar with it. This means they do not work as efficiently as they could. Often they have to interrupt the work of others to obtain assistance. This causes delays in routine work flows.

I propose that an intensive training programme be set up in order to help team members become proficient users of Microsoft Excel. This will help overcome the delays in work resulting from their unfamiliarity with the program.

For the team manager writing the proposal, the need for training is clear. Training will satisfy the demands of their team members and solve the problems caused by the team members' lack of expertise.

However, their immediate superior – the head of department (HoD) – to whom the proposal is to be put, may identify several contra-indicating factors. These might include:

1   Training costs money. One of my roles is to keep costs down and my reputation depends on being able to do so. Wouldn't one or two training manuals be an adequate alternative?

2   Teamwork and collaboration are integral to our company ethos. The communication and skills sharing that occur when team members support others with the use of software programs should therefore be viewed in a positive light.

Bearing in mind these potential arguments against their proposal, the Team Manager will need to decide whether it is worth the effort required to convince their HoD to agree to it. They might be concerned that it will undermine their team's position, especially if they have plans to raise other issues that will require their HoD's financial backing in the near future.

On the other hand, the team manager might decide that the issue is sufficiently important to persuade their HoD of its value. In that case, the manager will need to enter into a dialogue with their HoD and try to convince them otherwise. For each anticipated doubt or argument against the proposal, the team manager will need to provide a valid response or counter-argument to challenge and overcome it.

Before you look at the following response, return to the HoD's arguments and think what counter-arguments might be possible.

The table below contains some convincing responses to the reservations identified by the Team Manager's HoD.

Reservation argument	*Response counter-arguments*
1 Training costs money. One of my roles is to keep costs down and my reputation depends on being able to do so.	I understand that a training programme will cost money, but the delays caused by team members' lack of knowledge are becoming serious. The current design project has resulted in increased workloads, which means even small delays have a bigger impact. If we don't spend a relatively small amount of money on training, it will be necessary to take on another part-timer to deal with the workload, and that will incur even higher costs.
	I understand that your reputation depends on keeping costs down, but you may remember that recent statements from the Chairman focused on the need to provide development opportunities – such as training – to employees, in order to improve staff retention. With this in mind, the proposal could enhance your reputation and the efficiency of the department.
2 Teamwork and collaboration are integral to our company ethos. The communication and skills sharing that occurs when team members support others with the use of software programs should therefore be viewed in a positive light.	I understand the importance of encouraging collaboration within the company. However, as pressures increase on everyone's time, the need to interrupt others with requests for help is becoming a source of unease and tension rather than a positive opportunity for communication and skills sharing.
	Provision of training will overcome this problem and could result in an improved working environment.

Building an inner dialogue

Activity 6.19 ....

Purpose: to practise building an inner dialogue of reservation arguments and response counter-arguments in a proposal.

Task: choose one scenario from Activity 6.5 and imagine you want to present the suggested solution to your boss in a written proposal.

Create a table with the headings below.

Think about the people who will read the proposal and try to anticipate some of the reservations they might identify when they read it. List at least three of them in note form in the left-hand column.

Now consider what reasonable arguments you could use to respond to the reservations. Note these in the right-hand column.

Reservation argument	Response counter-argument

Activity 6.20 ....

Purpose: to practise building an inner dialogue of arguments and counter arguments in a workplace proposal.

Task: create another table like the one in Activity 6.19.

Look again at the mini-proposal you prepared for Online Activity 6.1. Think about the person who will read the proposal and try to anticipate some of the reservation arguments they might identify when they read it. Enter these in note form in the left-hand column of your table.

Then consider what reasonable response counter-arguments you could use to respond to them. Note these in the right-hand column.

Comment   ....

You will write these notes into your workplace proposal after the next activity.

In writing a convincing proposal you should anticipate any reservations your readers may have and integrate reasonable arguments to counter them.

There are two ways to do so: **explicitly** and **implicitly**. These are considered in turn next.

To do this **explicitly** means that you specify each of the arguments that you anticipate from your reader(s) and address them in turn, as in Extract I below, which is an extract from a longer proposal.

Extract I

It could be argued that training is expensive and that it may not be the best use of the company's limited resources. It might be suggested that the use of manuals would be sufficient in these circumstances. Purchasing these would be cheaper than implementing an extensive training programme. This would also avoid the need to arrange the release of staff for the duration of the course.

However, I do not believe that such an approach would be successful in this case. Team members are already under considerable time pressures and to expect them to read manuals and acquire new skills in an unsupervised way is likely to be resented. Such an approach may therefore prove ineffective in the long run.

Note that the inner dialogue of arguments and counter-arguments of a workplace proposal tries to anticipate some of the potential doubts of your reader. The use of **modal** verbs (*could*, *might*, etc.) reinforces three points. First, it shows that you are aware that there are people who may have different opinions from you. By recognising these opinions in your proposal, you are respecting these alternative views. Secondly, you may suspect it is the reader who has the alternative views, or there may be other people in the organisation with these reservations that the reader will be aware of. However, the modal verbs reinforce the sense that – in your view – these misgivings are hypothetical – and not necessarily valid concerns. Finally, the use of modal verbs also demonstrates that you have thought through your proposal carefully and this increases its credibility.

This language of interaction with the audience is referred to in Section D of the Influential Document Checklist. The next activity focuses on the way modal verbs are used.

Activity 6.21   ....

Purpose: to review the language of interaction with the reader and hypothesis.

Task: complete the table below with the relevant verb phrases from Extract I.

Subject	Verb	
It		be argued that ...
It		not be the best use of .
It		be suggested that ...
The use of manuals		be sufficient in these circumstances.
Purchasing these		be cheaper than implementing ...
This		also avoid the need to ...

There are no suggested answers for this activity because the answers are in Extract I.

Comment   ....

Note how **impersonal** modal constructions such as *It could be argued ...' It might be suggested ...'* are used to introduce potential reservation arguments against the proposal. These forms are much more likely to obtain the desired response than more personal expressions such as *You would probably argue that ...* which would identify the audience with these views in such a direct way that they might feel obliged to defend them rather than accept the response counter-argument.

As you can see, in Extract I the sentences of interaction are organised into two paragraphs which explicitly present the reservation arguments that the audience might have and then a full counter-argument in response to that. This pattern could be given the pattern: reservation-argument + response counter-argument. There are other ways to organise this kind of explicit interaction which are illustrated in the extracts below.

The following paragraph is organised with the pattern of proposal + reservation-argument + response counter-argument (positive–negative–positive). Mark the extract to show where each stage in the paragraph begins and ends.

Paragraph level

Proposal + reservation-argument + response counter-argument (positive–negative–positive)

An intensive training programme in the use of Microsoft Excel will help team members become proficient users and overcome delays in work resulting from their unfamiliarity with the program. There will be a cost associated with this, which will have to be met out of the departmental budget. However, this outlay on training will make it possible avoid the expense of employing an extra member of staff to deal with the current workload.

This pattern can also be observed at the sentence level. The organisation of the following sentences also follows a particular pattern. Mark the extracts to show where each stage in the sentences begins and ends.

Sentence level

Reservation-argument + connective + response counter-argument (negative–positive)

It would be more economical to introduce a self-training manual. However, this could be less effective, particularly for the staff who have been identified as having a training need.

Proposal + connective + reservation-argument + response counter-argument (positive–negative–positive)

The need for training is clear and, although it could be argued that there are other ways to tackle it, face-to-face training would be the most effective for the staff concerned.

Connective + reservation-argument + response counter-argument (negative–positive)

Although a training programme would require a special budget, we believe that this expense would be outweighed by the benefits to be gained in increased efficiency of working.

Activity 6.22

Purpose: to practise handling reservation arguments and response counter-arguments.

Task: take one of the reservation arguments to your proposal in Activity 6.19. Write two paragraphs, the first explaining the argument, the second providing the response counter-argument. Use modal verbs as necessary.

Then write the same information in a shorter form, using one of the sentence-level patterns above.

Comment

In writing a convincing workplace proposal, you should anticipate the possible reservations of your reader(s) and integrate reasonable counter-arguments in response. The methods you have practised so far make the reservations explicit.

Another way of addressing the possible reservations of your reader (s) is to do this **implicitly**. This means that, while you don't specifically refer to their anticipated reservation-argument against the proposal, you ensure that you bear it in mind and use a response counter-argument that would answer anyone with such a reservation. In effect, this is a way of emphasising the benefits of the proposal.

For example:

Explicit

It could be argued that face-to-face training will cost too much; however, that financial cost has to be offset against the cost in efficiency of not providing training in the most effective form.

Implicit

Training in the most effective form for the employees concerned will ensure more efficient working and economic gains for the company.

Activity 6.23 ....

Purpose: to practise addressing the possible reservations of your reader(s) implicitly by integrating response counter-arguments into your proposal.

Task: redraft the text you wrote in Activity 6.22 to build in implicit response arguments.

6.4 Writing a proposal for an attendance management procedure

Activity 6.24 ....

Purpose: to practise writing a workplace proposal.

Task: Text 6.3 in Resource Book 3 reports on the implementation of a solution to a workplace problem.

Read the text carefully. Then imagine that you are the member of staff in Human Resources who originally recommended the solution to Tesco's Board of Directors.

Using the functions list (Table 6.1) as a reference point, draft the content of your written proposal. Then redraft it – based on the Influential Document Checklist – until it is in a finished form.

There is no suggested answer for this activity.

6.5 Writing a proposal for a training initiative

Activity 6.25 ....

Purpose: to use the language skills and knowledge developed during this session to write a workplace proposal.

Task: imagine that you work in the human resources (HR) department of a company. This department has done some research across the company and identified a range of problems arising from poor written communication skills. Training in the company is paid for out of individual departmental budgets, therefore it is necessary for all departments to support the decision to set up any training. The head of HR asks you to write a proposal to be circulated to all department heads. This will make a case for setting up a training programme in written communication skills and for departments to contribute to the cost of it as well as support their staff's attendance.

You are free to imagine a company of any size and in any sector for this activity. You should briefly describe your imaginary company as the context for the proposal in an introductory paragraph. This paragraph will give your tutor the context for the document and is not part of the proposal.

You can use information from any part of this book in writing your proposal. You may find Sessions 2 and 4 are particularly relevant. (This includes the material you wrote for Activity 4.14, although you should not concentrate solely on email communication in this task.) You may want to obtain further information from the internet on companies which specialise in corporate communications training.

Use the functions list in Figure 6.1 as a reference point and refer to the Influential Document Checklist to help with your writing.

6.6 Review

In this session you should have:

- gained an understanding of the function of workplace proposals
- developed your skill in writing the different functional parts of workplace proposals
- learned to analyse situations in terms of problems and solutions
- familiarised yourself with the possible structures of workplace proposals
- focused on the language that makes them effective
- written your own workplace proposal.

6.7 Critical reflection

This session explains how to create an inner dialogue with the reader of your proposal, by anticipating and responding to their possible reservations. In your Learning Journal reflect on the following questions: What do you think of this technique? Are there other situations where it might be useful?

Compare your knowledge of workplace proposal writing at the beginning of this session with that you have gained now that you are at the end. What have you found to be most valuable? What do you feel less confident about?

6.8 Conclusion

Successful writers manage the content, organisation and language of the texts they write to fulfil particular purposes and engage with particular readers. This principle is the same for academic and business environments. The aim of this book was to show how written communication skills which are developed in business studies can be adapted to communication in the workplace.

The course as a whole has focused on some of the features which make texts work in particular environments. The text structures, sentence patterns and vocabulary choices you have studied are used because they work for particular purposes and with particular readers.

Becoming a successful communicator means developing your awareness of what these successful texts are like and using this awareness to create successful texts of your own. The goal of this course was to help you extend such knowledge and skills. We hope you will be able to build on what you have learned here and continue to develop as a successful communicator in both business studies and your workplace. We wish you success.

6.9 Answer section

Activity 6.1

1 D; 2 E; 3 F; 4 A; 5 B; 6 C.

Other examples of persuasion verbs:
win over, sway, urge, advise, suggest, propose.

Activity 6.3

2   The goal is to standardise the company's procedures and ensure its good reputation.

3   The goal is to combat negative critique of the company's poor salaries.

4   The goal is to maintain the company's revenue and ensure its survival.

5   The goal is to improve the company's reputation and to raise its success and profit in the places where it expands.

6   The goal is to increase profit by catering to the special needs of the target population.

Activity 6.4

(a)   The problem (P): absenteeism in training sessions.

(b)   The beneficial goal (G): to establish the reasons for absenteeism (**not** to *provide training of relevance to staff*, which is a more general goal).

(c)   The solution that is being proposed (S): investigation into patterns and causes of absenteeism by phased collection of information.

(d)   The action is internal (I).

Activity 6.9

Task 1

Text 6.1
General goal statement: Our goal is to provide training of relevance to our employees and their work and to ensure that they get the maximum benefit from participation. **Specific goal statement**: we need to know what the true level of attendance is and what factors contribute to non-attendance

Text 6.2
General goal statement: to draw attention to the unique potential of Department X and how it could be developed to become a more productive department.

Activity 6.10

(a) (P) Our organisation currently lacks a disaster plan.

(b) (C) and (E): the organisation has not taken every precaution for the safety and security of our staff; runs the risk of being severely disrupted; could be held responsible for any deaths and injuries; may already be losing business.

(c) (G) It is now becoming more frequent for businesses to have plans to put into action in the event of disasters such as fire, flood, disease and terrorism. This implies the goal is to be an organisation with a disaster plan.

(d) (S) A disaster plan should be produced with some urgency.

Activity 6.11

Task 1
The writer of Extract C probably decided to use (d).

It is	recommended	that	a disaster plan	be	produced.

because a recommendation is a strong statement of authority. If the other, more personal recommendation statements are used, the authority of the writer is stated very directly. By using this more formal statement, the *you* and *I* relationship is not highlighted and the readers are freer to decide for or against the recommendation.

Task 2
Extract D is not exactly the same as statement (d), but it is the closest.

Activity 6.12

(a) (P) On several occasions, it has been unclear whether or not a specific document has in fact been sent out to our clients. (b) (E) This has sometimes led to embarrassment and could jeopardise our long-term relationship with them. It also means that considerable time and energy are spent in tracking the document in question. (c) (G) It is important that all our documents can be tracked efficiently so that this kind of uncertainty does not occur in future. (e) (S) It is therefore recommended that a document log be created for this purpose.

Activity 6.15

Task 1

Each step includes the goal or benefit that will be obtained from carrying out the step. Steps 1 and 3 use the connective *in order to* to connect the step with the goal or benefit. Step 2 uses the verb *to determine* to do the same.

Task 2

Recommendation 2 has three steps: staff should be completely familiarised with the procedure manual; they should make direct contact with both the Department X buyer and the various vendors; they should spend time with the customer, answering, asking and anticipating questions.

Recommendation 4 has three steps: create a new Department X separate from the Linens Department; develop a regular staff of Sales Associates for the new department; pay regular staff of the new department on a part-commission basis.

Activity 6.17

Threats: conservative attitude toward spending, shopping more carefully, considering their purchases thoughtfully, trying to get as much for their money as possible, spending as little of it as possible.

Opportunities: used to develop the sales potential; offers a very real alternative to the expense of; the limitation of [what?].

Weaknesses: potential cannot be realised, is poorly organised and staffed by inadequately trained personnel.

Potential *Strengths*: an efficiently structured department; a core of professional, competent and knowledgeable Sales Associates could offer a large selection, good quality, be able to answer questions, begin to realise its full potential; make an increased contribution.

Activity 6.18

Text 6.2 ends with a very clear SWOT evaluation demonstrating the benefits of the proposal. This proposal does not contain a direct call to action probably because it was not requested by the organisation's chairperson. It comes from the writer's own initiative, so it is probably too early to call the organisation to action. The organisation needs time to think about the proposal first.

References

Arnold, J., Cooper, C. L. and Robertson, I. T. (1995) *Work Psychology: Understanding Human Behaviour in the Workplace* (2nd edn), London, Pitman.

Doherty, M., Knapp, L. and Swift, S. (1987) *Write for Business*, Harlow, Longman.

Fairclough, N. (1992) *Discourse and Social Change*, Cambridge, Polity Press.

Hofstede, G. (2001) *Culture's Consequences* (2nd edn), Thousand Oaks, CA, Sage.

Shannon, C.E. and Weaver, W. (1949) *A Mathematical Model of Communication*, Urbana, IL, University of Illinois Press.

Acknowledgements

Grateful acknowledgement is made to the following sources:

Text

Page 120, Extract A: from http://www.nokia.com/NOKIA_COM_1/About_Nokia/Financials/Quarterley_and_Annual_information/Q1_2006/results2006Q1e.pdf; pages 167–8: Influential Document Checklist, The University of Sydney, 1997, 'MASUS project'.

Tables

Page 121, Table 5.1: www.nokia.com, 2007.

Illustrations

Page 7: © Getty Images/Photodisc; page 66, Figure 3.2: Arnold, J. Cooper, C.L. and Robertson, I.T. (1995) *Work Psychology: Understanding Human Behaviour in the Workplace* (2nd edn), Pitman; page 103: © Travelshots.com/Alamy; page 107: © Paul Doyle/Alamy; page 113: © Getty Images/Photodisc; page 124: © Bruno Budrovic @ Getty images; page 136: © Getty Images/Photodisc.

Appendix   Influential Document Checklist

Criteria

A Research

Are the research procedures appropriate for the task and used effectively to create the text?

1   Appropriate research methods are used
2   Relevant information from research is used
3   Information from research is integrated into text effectively
4   Plagiarism is avoided
5   Bibliography or reference list is constructed correctly

B Organisation of the text

Is the structure of the text clear and appropriate to the task and the context?

1   Overall text structure is appropriate to the task
2   Stages of the text are sequenced appropriately
3   Information is distributed appropriately through the stages
4   High-level generalisations organise text
5   Text is appropriately concise
6   Headings, numberings and bullet points reinforce the organisation
7   Visuals are used appropriately

C Language of the field

Is the language appropriate for the subject of the text?

1   Appropriate choice of technical words
2   Appropriate choice of non-technical words
3   Appropriate use of abstract words
4   Appropriate combinations of words
5   Appropriate language of description, analysis and evaluation

D Language of the relationship

Is the language appropriate for the audience and the reader–writer relationship?

1   Correct identification of audience
2   Effective adjustment to reader knowledge
3   Recognition of different viewpoints
4   Appropriate level of formality
5   Appropriate level of interaction (or dialogue) with reader
6   Appropriate use of evaluation language
7   Appropriate use of pronouns in reader–writer relationship
8   Writer identity (or voice) is established effectively

E Language of text organisation

Does the language reinforce the organisation of the text?

1   Themes of text, sections, paragraphs and sentences show what they are about

2   Themes are linked appropriately to what has gone before

3   Text, sections, paragraphs and sentences have a point

4   Connectives reinforce the organisation of the information

F Qualities of presentation

1   Clause structure follows recognisable and appropriate patterns of English

2   Consistent and appropriate tense choice, correctly formed

3   Spelling generally correct

4   Word processing appropriate

5   Punctuation used appropriately

(Source: adapted from materials created by the MASUS Project, *The MASUS Procedure: Diagnostic Assessment of Literacy Skills: A Resource Pack*, The University of Sydney, 1997, with permission)

Index

Entries in **bold type** are defined in the course Glossary.